Beating the 1
in
Georgian Norwich

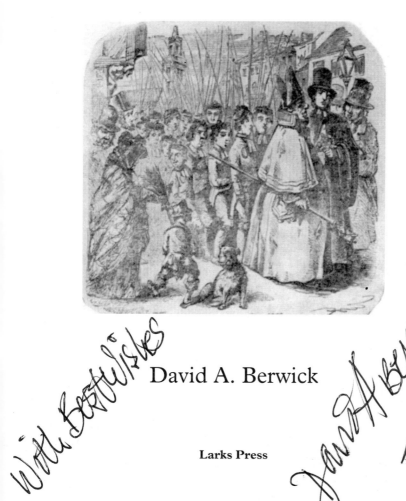

David A. Berwick

Larks Press

Published by the Larks Press
Ordnance Farmhouse, Guist Bottom
Dereham NR20 5PF
01328 829207
www.booksatlarkspress.co.uk

Printed by Lanceni Press, Garrood Drive, Fakenham

★★★

This book is dedicated to the memory of my late mother,

Elsie Hilda Berwick

who died September 2005.
She cherished all aspects of the history of this Fine City, and greatly
encouraged me in my researches over many a long year.

★★★

Acknowledgements
My grateful thanks are extended to the very helpful staff of the Norfolk
Record Office, both in the new Archive Centre at County Hall, and at the
previous old City Central Library.
Also my warm thanks to John Renton, Curator of Collections Norfolk
Museums and Archaeology Service, (Bridewell Museum) and to his former
colleague there, David Jones.
I am also indebted to Katherine d'Este Hoare, Historic Buildings Project
Officer, City Hall, Norwich, for her time and helpfulness.
For the hours of wrestling with my endless demands and detailed
typographic design features (not to mention regular computer trouble-
shooting) and for the front cover design I thank my son Stephen most
heartily.
I also gladly acknowledge the very helpful photographic assistance given to
me by Laura Bishop.

ISBN 978 1 904006 35 3

Contents

Front cover shows a parish boundary plate for St George Tombland dated 1777

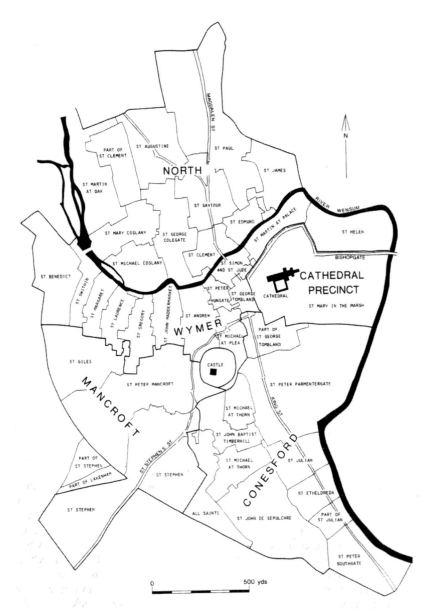

Parish Boundaries in the City of Norwich

This map shows the large number of small parishes in the City,
especially close to the river. Though small in area, many parishes were rich
in tithes and properties paying poor rates, so marking the boundaries was
very important, hence the care taken to beat the bounds at regular intervals.

Introduction

Is it surprising that we still possess so many of our ancient central city buildings in Norwich? Perhaps it is. However, the historic sky-line has yielded in some measure to the unavoidable development of the last sixty years. Buildings have disappeared, and with them went many examples of important fixtures and fittings. Typical of this lost 'street furniture' are considerable numbers of 18th and 19th century parish boundary markers from central Norwich.

In 1934, a public-minded citizen, a Mr J.E. Read, conducted a small-scale survey of all the then known boundary markers. His findings were brought to my attention in 1980 and this in-depth research, now published, is the most complete on the subject undertaken since then. On 17th April 1934 the *Eastern Daily Press* carried an article by Mr Read under the title 'Beating the Bounds - Rogation Day Custom in Norwich'. This very interesting contribution provoked some illuminating correspondence from EDP readers. Another article by Mr Read was published in the EDP three months later on 26 July.

(Joseph Edward Read was born in 1851 in Lakenham, Norwich, and died in 1936, only one year after his final EDP article.)

Within his first submission Mr Read included a list of locations where it was still possible to view various boundary markers. By the time the second item was published, the list (thanks to the interest of EDP readers) had grown from eighty boundary markers to one hundred and forty.

In November 1934, after much diligent research, Mr Read could report the existence of one hundred and sixty markers. By early 1935 the total had reached two hundred and five. Once embarked on, this most fascinating subject obviously became very difficult for him to leave alone. I have found it so myself – hence, at last, this book.

Sadly, of that considerable total of markers extant in 1935 only ninety remain today on public buildings. Even more to be regretted is the fact that four parishes, which had marker plates in 1935, are no longer represented in the Norwich boundary marker record, as all their examples (identified on page 5) have since disappeared. The notes and some photographs, which were used as copy for the EDP articles, were subsequently very carefully hand-bound into covers on vellum by Mr Read. His work has all the appearance of an enthusiast's scrapbook. However, the modest exterior belies its value. The book contains fascinating, if fading, black and white photographs (which I suspect he processed himself) plus some detailed notes. I first studied its pages in the early 1980s. Thankfully it survived the devastating fire in Norwich Library on 1 August 1994.

Mr Read was not to know how timely his survey findings were to be. Within half a decade Norwich was subjected first to three years of continual

1

bomb damage, then to many more of post-war city-centre development. Buildings were flattened and parish boundary markers were lost with them.

We should be thankful that some plates were rescued. Often this came about because concerned parishioners alerted the clearance teams to their position. However, many a lead marker plate must literally have melted away forever on buildings burnt by enemy action. A few that were miraculously saved are those to be found today amongst the Bridewell Museum collection. Even though many have no precise rescue-site information, their survival at all under the circumstances is remarkable.

During the twenty-five years it has taken me to research this book and conduct my own detailed survey of all our city buildings, there have been numerous occasions when markers went missing during demolition work. Thankfully we are blessed in Norwich with a Museum Service actively engaged in the rescue of historical artefacts when the call for such action arises.

Mr David Jones, Keeper of Social History in the early 1980s, put much effort into the rescue of threatened markers. His timely intervention on several occasions was vital and a number of markers were placed within the Museum Service for safe keeping. Others removed by developers have reappeared on replacement buildings. An example of careful storage and later re-fixing on a new building occurred in Westlegate when Norwich Union Insurance Group (NU) redeveloped in that street.

In April 1981 I wrote to the Society to express concern for the safety of a boundary plate for 1818 (All Saints Parish) on a building due for demolition. The NU Estates Department confirmed they had the plate safe and would be putting it back. In June 1983 the plate was indeed back in Westlegate mounted on the new building in approximately the original position. A satisfactory outcome

1983 also witnessed the temporary loss, and subsequent recovery, of three plates illegally removed during a much publicised and controversial partial demolition in Calvert Street. After several frantic phone calls by myself and the Museums Service, the 'lost' plates (St Saviour's 1801, 1816 & 1832) were located, recovered, and placed safely in the Bridewell Museum. The demolition firm concerned was duly prosecuted. It is a pity, however, that the plates have never been reinstated in their correct location on the new building. I am hoping that my published research and other initiatives will encourage reinstatement in the future at this and other sites.

In 1994 the disappearance of three plates from a site in Pitt Street was rather worrying. I had been keeping an eye on this building, which was being extensively refurbished. I made contact on the site with the owner, Mr Tetlow (then of Morris Printing Company). He was also very enthusiastic about local history and had every intention of repositioning the plates later. However, complaints elsewhere had already reached City Hall. Official correspondence ensued demanding the re-fixing of the markers.

I was happy to take up the offer of a thorough inspection of all three plates. It was thrilling actually handling these early 19th century items, before they were carefully cleaned and returned to their original positions. This impressive site is well worth visiting.

Shortly before this book went to press, disconcerting news broke of the impending sale of a Norwich boundary marker. I was told the plate belonged to the year 1748 and bore the initials St GTL. My records revealed that this was a year represented in the Norwich collection by only two other plates. Sadly, neither myself nor the Priest in Charge of St George Tombland could persuade the auctioneers in Yorkshire to halt proceedings. Neither were they particularly impressed by our assertions that this item could only be legally owned by the original parish. They had in fact correctly stated in their catalogue that it came from the parish of St George Tombland, Norwich. Further, they explained the meaning of 'Tombland' to their readers, so they could not claim ignorance of the importance and rarity of what they were selling, and they should not have ignored my demand that they return the item to Norwich. Sadly, our Museums Service was not able to assist owing to lack of funds. In spite of all pleading, the sale went ahead. A very unsatisfactory outcome. Details for this plate will be found in Appendix D classed as 'precise whereabouts unknown'.

To the uninitiated eye, some of the markers are not very striking and their true purpose and importance is not at all obvious. I hope that the publication of this modest book will sharpen awareness of these important artefacts, and help to ensure their safe survival.

The following chapters describe how and why the boundary markers were put in place, how they were made, and by whom, together with pictures of the various types of marker still to be found. An attempt will also be made to convey the colourful festive atmosphere that accompanied the fixing up of the markers around our city streets.

I have already commented on the sad fact that many central city buildings have vanished forever. It is even more galling that we know some of them had boundary markers fixed on them. These setbacks in research have been occasionally offset by the excitement of discovering parish plates not known to have existed back in 1934. Only very recently I found plates not previously recorded when checking the rear of buildings in St Giles Street and Queen's Street, the last after a fruitful tip-off from the Conservation Department at City Hall, following my contact there with Philip Insley.

In connection with discoveries, I will always remember July 1983 when I went to the Bridewell Museum in Norwich. I had been granted permission to look behind the scenes to note any boundary plates they had in store. That day proved to be rewarding and amazing. I had been led to believe that 'there might be a few markers'. Twenty-eight were produced. A number of these were previously noted in Mr Read's 1934 survey, and subsequently thought to be lost for all time.

The majority of these items bore no reference to the exact site they had been removed from, which was a pity. Never mind, they had been 'found' and the subsequent handling and inspection I gave them that day was an exhilarating and humbling experience. The rediscovery of this number of markers led to a significant adjustment to the card index I was preparing at the time.

I had long thought it likely that large parishes would put up considerable numbers of plates. Here were plates whose reverse sides were punched XIII and one example XXIII. This plate was for St Mary Coslany 1812. I had made sure that these were not museum marks so they had to be original numerals struck by the makers. Intriguing! The whole question of how many markers were put in place during a parish boundary perambulation is discussed at greater length in Chapter Two.

Two markers of equal interest to me also came to light that day. The survey conducted by Mr Read back in 1934/35 had noted that a plate was to be seen then fixed on number 15, Golden Dog Lane, off Magdalen Street. (See Appendix A). Sadly, this plate was no longer to be found at that location when I inspected the site. But here, in the archives of the Museums Service, was a plate

4

for St George Colegate, for the year 1821, bearing a note on the reverse to indicate that it came from 'Golden Dog Lane'. Very likely it was the same plate.

The other marker to particularly delight me that day was one definitely seen and annotated by Mr Read. In his article in the EDP for 26 July 1934 he comments '... the plate dated 1729, taken from St Martin's Lane is the oldest lead plate. It is made of a flat sheet of lead, with the lettering pierced through, instead of the usual casting with raised figures. Being fragile, it is now preserved by being mounted on an oak board. It was a St Michael Coslany Boundary mark.'

Close inspection showed me just what an intricate task the original maker had creating cut-outs of such quality. No doubt this effort had to be multiplied perhaps a dozen times as well.

Mr Read does not pinpoint exactly where he saw this plate. Maybe it was one of the markers he knew to be in the care of what was known then as the City Engineers Department, having been previously removed by them from demolition areas. Anyway, here, still safe, was *the* plate in the Bridewell Museum. It is very delicate and thank goodness someone took that safeguarding action all those years ago to protect it by mounting it on a sturdy wooden block.

In his valuable notebook Mr Read records all the years known from the 1710-1854 era which had markers still extant in 1934. This is a most enlightening observation, as I could work out from this list just how many years and parishes were now lost from the complete inventory of Boundary Beating events in that span of years. Regrettably, 18 recorded years have vanished up to 2006. Even worse, within this total were parishes for which we now have no plates whatever in existence. Those parishes now missing from his 1934 list are: 1756 & 1827 (St Martin-at-Palace); 1817 & 1831 (Hamlet of Pockthorpe); 1824 & 1837 (St James Pockthorpe) and 1837 (St Paul).

When Mr Read was himself perambulating the whole city, notebook in hand and camera at the ready, he knew he was engaged on a subject of great interest and value. I feel he already had fears that the plates existing in 1934 were vulnerable. His interest aroused in others a similar pride in these important items. According to his daughter, Mrs Eastoe, writing in *The East Anglian Magazine* in July 1958, her father's actions saved many plates then under threat. His work certainly encouraged me to pick up the baton half a century later. Even though they are sparse, I am proud to publish his findings in this book. (See Appendix A).

I hope that readers will enjoy my book and will find within its pages enough of interest to provoke them to care more for the historic buildings and artefacts around them, and be proactive towards their preservation for those who follow us. If you happen to find an 'unknown' boundary marker I would like to hear about it. Please contact me via the publisher.

David A. Berwick
Norwich 2007.

Perhaps the most impressive surviving parish boundary marker site in Norwich. It will be found at the Coach & Horses public house on Bethel Street.

The impressive display of four parish boundary plates to be found at number 4 Princes Street, Norwich. Those on the left are for the Parish of St Andrew, and those facing for St Peter Hungate.

CHAPTER ONE

Beating the Bounds in City and County
Origin, Customs & Traditions.

The consensus of opinion is that ancient Romans were the first people to make an annual ceremonial procession to mark a pagan rite. Their celebration, called the *Robigalia,* was to honour the god Robigus, who they thought could protect their crops from developing a destructive mould, called *robigo.* The festival day fell on 25th April and the procession was to his shrine on the outskirts of Rome. The event was marked with sports and other activities. Some were rather gross, and involved animal sacrifice. The early Christian church did not approve of this behaviour and, over time, converted the annual observance into one based on prayer and supplication.

It is likely that the Christian origin of following, or 'beating' the parish or town boundaries, dates from about AD 470. It was then that St Marmertus, the Bishop of Vienne, a region near Lyon in France, decided to perambulate the regional border to ward off the recurrence of recently-endured severe weather and earthquakes. In due course, the Rogation Days in the Church calendar came to be those most often used for this ritual. From its Latin source the meaning of 'rogation' is a plea, an asking of the Almighty, to implore His protection of the germinating seeds for the forthcoming harvest. Good weather for gathering grain and fruit in due season was also prayed for at this time. It was therefore adopted as the natural season for circuiting the boundaries of a parish. This was certainly so in Georgian Norwich. The Rogation Days are those after Easter, and immediately prior to the Ascension, which itself is 40 days after Easter Day. Ascension Day, always a Thursday, was often reserved for the parish 'perambulation'. However, parishioners in 18th century Norwich did not strictly observe this. I have calculated that other days of the week were used, even a Sunday in one case.

Beating the bounds was a means of stimulating a memory map in the minds of the followers. This would be important in the settlement of any future territorial disputes. There was a strong belief that observing the boundary by special procession would not only be an opportunity to thank God for His goodness, but would also allow for good relations with one's neighbours. Being charitable towards the poor and destitute at this time was also encouraged.

The development of the annual boundary-beating custom saw it come to be called by other names. 'Perambulation' was much favoured in Georgian Norwich together with 'Going the Bounds'. In other parts of the country we find terms such as 'Gang Days' and 'Cross Days', both of these deriving from gatherings of people (gangs) following the holy cross in procession. It is thought likely that the expressions 'Gospel Oak' and 'Amen Corner', amongst others, came into common usage, owing to sermons being preached at a certain boundary point, often an oak tree. Parish boundary beating is still carried out today in a limited way, in villages towns and cities in the U.K. In the 18th and 19th centuries coin-shaped commemorative tokens were sometimes distributed to the boundary walkers. Another custom saw the introduction of 'Rammalation Biscuits' (obviously a corruption of Perambulation). They are still eaten in some parts of the country, although there seems to be no particular recipe. The Tower of London occasionally marks its boundary by a procession, following a religious ceremony.

Beating the village bounds in rural areas was just as important as in towns and cities. An interesting countryside account appeared in the *East Anglian Magazine* in 1958. It describes in detail the perambulation of the parish boundary surrounding the village of Mendlesham in Suffolk, in the year 1898.

The account was written by a Mr Walter Tye who himself was amongst the 'beaters' that day. It is a lovely story, and it is not difficult to imagine the walking party having a certain excitement and anticipation about them, on such a special day.

We are told the titles and occupations of some of the people. The evidence of a rather fuzzy photograph would suggest all were males. The ages appear to range from a young lad of about eight to an elderly gentleman in his seventies. In all, some thirty people took part and enjoyed the company of good friends with a common goal in mind. A fascinating event and one that would live on as a clear recollection for each and every participant. Of course, it was meant to. 'Imprinting' the memory, was vitally important.

This is Mr Tye's very interesting account of the perambulation of 1898 (recalled in 1958).

I well remember 'beating the bounds' of Mendlesham some 60 years ago in 1898. From all accounts it has only been repeated once since, in 1913.

Being a large parish of about 4,000 acres, with a boundary almost 10 miles long, it took the better part of the day to get round it. The hedges were thick and tall, the ditches wide and the land sticky, as most land is in High Suffolk. Old Suffolkers often describe it as 'rather drably bor'. The 'beaters' assembled at a point in the boundary along the Brockford Road, barely half a mile from 'The Street' the recognised centre of Mendlesham's scattered community. The party included the churchwardens, the parish surveyor, the leading farmers and tradesmen and the village schoolmaster, then the instigator and organiser of all social affairs in the district. To him we also looked for an explanation of all things both ancient and modern. Then there was the village policeman, who gave the affair a semblance of

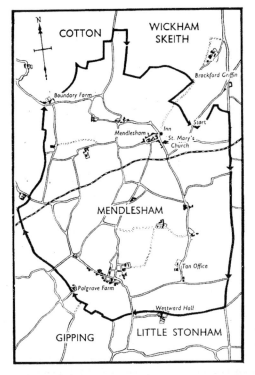

authority. I cannot recall any farm labourers being present; most likely they could not afford to take a day off.

Most of the 'beaters' turned out in hefty 'home-made' boots, well fitting leather buskins, corduroy breeches and a sort of Victorian sports jacket, well lined with useful pockets. Ash sticks were cut out of the hedges, and very useful they were too, to beat a way through hedge, ditch and row. Mendlesham hedges those days took some getting through, especially in the old Hundred lanes, where in places they met overhead.

After having our photographs taken, a rare occurrence in the 1890s, we set out across the fields, following the boundary to the main Norwich

to Ipswich Road, sometimes spoken of as the turnpike, but more often 'The Great Rud'. On our left, not far from the boundary, was Brockford Griffin, a tempting place for a call, but the leader decided otherwise. No need to look at the map for a time, for the boundary ran straight along the turnpike towards Ipswich. Very little traffic was seen, except a few slow going tumbrels and an occasional farmer's gig. Discussion turned on the wayside farms and the proposed Mid-Suffolk Light Railway. Little did we think in those far off days that some of us would live long enough to see that quaint little railway, locally known as the 'Mad Suffolk', come and go. Plodding along we then discussed the latest trotting races, which were often seen on the turnpike during the '80s and '90s. These races, which usually took place on Sundays, drew big crowds from the nearby villages. The course, about 20 miles, mostly laid between Barham Sorrel House and Thwaite Buck's Head, two well-known Suffolk inns. Accompanying the trotting horses and gigs were a number of judges mounted on horse-back. Should any competitor allow his horse to break into a gallop, he was immediately ordered to stop and turn horse and gig completely round, before continuing the race. On arriving at a mile-stone we were suddenly reminded of the actual purpose of the 'beat', to impress on the young where the boundary ran. Two or three of the old hands seized a novice, lifted him shoulder high and somewhat forcibly bumped him on the mile-stone. Others received similar initiation, without much resistance, obviously the best policy. One or two, however, were upended at the next sign-post, a little further along the road.

Leaving the turnpike the leader, closely scrutinising the map, led us across country towards the old Hundred Lane, which separates Hartismere from the Gipping Hundred. Hawthorn hedges and stiff clay made the going hard. Evidently in olden days a small boy was often thrown over the thickest of the hedges, the 'beaters' passing through a nearby gap.

When approaching Westward Hall, the leader reminded us of a small remote hamlet on our right, called the Tan Office where, so said the old inhabitants, a Quakers' Meeting House existed until the middle of the last century. Could anyone imagine a more suitable place for worship and reflection? Maybe the Five Mile Act decided its whereabouts.

The boundary then took us through the premises of Westward Hall where, according to the map, we should have waded through a pond. The leader evidently thought it discreet to by-pass it and keep to dry land.

At last we struck the Hundred Lane, the most lonely and romantic stretch of the 'beat'. Nothing much was ever seen there except flocks of sheep and gipsy encampments. The Lees and Robinsons were frequent visitors in the 1890s. The lane, over a mile long, had but one house, Palgrave Farm, where I spent my early childhood. I can still recall the happy family gatherings of the gipsies, sitting smoking round the campfires at twilight. The smell of wood fires and their savoury cooking pots is unforgettable.

Trudging through the lane, conversation veered round to an ancient legend that 'Bloody Queen Mary' drove headless horses down the lane every night on her way to Gipping Hall, where her collaborator, Sir Edmund Tyrrell, lived. One old 'beater' vowed he knew it was true, as some hurdles he had put up across the lane, to keep the sheep in, were found knocked down next morning.

10

Boundary Farm

The most difficult obstacle encountered in the perambulation was a pig-sty at the Boundary Farm, through which everybody had to clamber, as it laid across the boundary. Entrance by the front gate was easy, but squeezing through the small muck-hole at the back was indeed trying, especially to the more corpulent farmers. Anyhow, with assistance both fore and aft, everybody managed to squeeze through. Most likely the expectancy of hospitality in the farm kitchen made everybody all the keener. And we were not disappointed. Never were ham sandwiches, pork pies, Suffolk rusks and home-brewed beer more relished. The beer, so said our host, was brewed on the day his eldest son was born, and he was in his teens. Despite caution, however, many of the thirsty 'beaters' were afterwards found sleeping it off in a haystack.

The last stretch took us over field after field of heavy soil and high hedges. The only building visible was the village church, peering over the high trees encompassing it. Here the map was constantly in use, for the boundary ran zig-zag alongside corn-fields and meadows. Many a dispute must have arisen between the inhabitants of Mendlesham and Wickham Skeith before ordnance maps came into use. Maybe this accounted for the strong antagonism that existed between these two parishes, even as late as the 1890s, when no young man dared risk looking for a sweetheart over the boundary. Fleeing from a gang of angry youths, with pockets full of stones, was a strong deterrent to the most ardent lover.

The 'beat' finished where we started, having taken us about seven hours to walk the boundary and enjoy an alfresco lunch. The photograph taken before we dispersed revealed that some who started did not finish - they were still dreaming on the haystack.

There were no absentees, however, at the Royal Oak Inn later in the day, when a sumptuous supper was laid out on long tables in an upper room. There before us were huge joints of beef and mutton, tasty pies, bowls of vegetables and salads, cakes of every description, and scores of shaky tinted jellies, the likes of which we seldom see today. Even if the aged Rector had failed to bless the crops during the day he certainly had no compunction in giving thanks for such a welcome spread. Supper was followed by speeches, songs, tales and jokes, most of which we had heard before, and of which we never tired. Farmers, tradesmen, millers, shoemakers, all took part, until we heard that oft repeated call, 'Time, gentlemen, please'. One and all agreed that 'beating the bounds' was a fine institution and should long continue. But alas, with the passage of time, this ancient custom is well *nigh forgotten, the Royal Oak Inn is no more and only a few of the old Mendlesham 'beaters' are left to tell the tale.*

★ ★ ★

Drinking considerable quantities of ale during these events (as described in the Mendlesham perambulation above) was also typical of Georgian boundary beating in Norwich. Very large expenditure features on some occasions, even when the church accounts make it obvious that some parishes could ill afford anything like the expense. (See Chapter Three).

Contemporary information about Norwich and its environs suggests that the general observance of this fascinating custom has lapsed. Only the central parish of Saint Peter Mancroft still occasionally perambulates a portion of its boundary. Choirboys even get the customary 'bumps' on the boundary of the Coach & Horses public house, in Bethel Street. Of which, more later.

The following city version of such an observance, unearthed during research, compares nicely with that of the rural parish of Mendlesham. In 1905, the Revd Dundas Harford, M.A., the Vicar of St Stephen's, Norwich, published a very interesting little book titled *A Norwich Parish 500 years ago.* Revd Harford had a rather fertile imagination. Nevertheless he creates an interesting little story.

Amongst the topics he touches upon is an imaginary account of a tour around the boundary of St Stephen's parish in 1405. The story is told in a quaint style but reads well for all that. The writer mixes fact and fiction by noting parish boundary markers still extant in his parish in 1905, then guessing what the scene would have been like on an early fifteenth century perambulation. Although it has none of the authority of the St Andrew's 1762 walk (see Chapter Two), it does note exactly where St Stephen's parish boundary markers were placed in 1905. The existence of markers in 1405 is doubtful, but the writer does mix in one necessary ingredient important on boundary walks - impressing the event on the minds of the followers. Conspicuously absent, however, is any reference to refreshments - especially visits to hostelries along the way. The Lame Dog only gets a passing mention.

Mature readers will warm to references of Messrs Bunting's shop and also the tram lines in Orford Place leading into Orford Hill. The oft-used term 'lead' relates to a boundary plate of course. None remain today along the route described where the boundary can still be identified. However, sited on the boundary line of this parish, plates may still be found on the rear of the Assembly House and also at 1, The Crescent, Chapelfield Road. Here is the creative account of Revd Dundas Harford M.A. back in 1905.

Beating the bounds.

Formerly it was the custom to take some small boys with the party which was to go round the parish, and to impress the debatable points of the boundaries upon their memories by such means as should awaken tender recollections in their minds, whenever they might subsequently pass those spots. Failing that let us start on our tour with such a company as may have perambulated the parish in the year 1405. The 'Good Vicar' is accompanied by two leading men of the city, Robert Brasier and John Daniel, both of whom had been Bailiffs of Norwich in 1403, and had on the appointment of the first Mayor in 1404 been elected as the first two Sheriffs. They had gone out of office probably at Michaelmas, but were both shortly to be chosen to the higher dignity of Mayor, in 1407 and 1410 respectively.

With us is also another Daniel, John's brother Walter, who was to succeed to the Mayoralty in the very next year (1406), and again in 1409. Mr Thomas Cock, the mercer, buried here in 1428, Sheriff in 1414, is perhaps in the company; and, who shall say, Mr Thomas Bokenham, buried here in 1460, may have at this date (fifty-five years before) been of a suitable age for that purpose to which allusion has already been made. In any case, look at any picture of the Canterbury pilgrims, and you may see in them, and in the lookers-on, types of the company in which we are now supposing ourselves to be.

Setting out then from the north porch of the church, we cross the Horse Market (Rampant Horse Street), and go a few yards down Church Street to where we now see the 'leads' on the right hand wall. There we turn to the right, and cross Abraham's Hall, where the Jews in the middle ages carried on the banking business still represented on the site. Coming out into Brigg Street, then a much more important thoroughfare than now (note the 'lead'), we turn to our left (along the tram lines through Orford Place to Orford Hill), passing on our right the Brasiers' bell foundry, either already or soon after established on this spot.

Half-way up the hill we find another 'lead'. Impress it on the 'memories' of those boys! Here the line runs a short way due south, zigzags to and fro at the back of Red Lion Street, and comes out into St Stephen's Plain, marching with the bounds of All Saints' parish; next crosses south-east (see 'lead') opposite Messrs Bunting's door, and, perhaps following the course of the 'Cockey', an ancient watercourse, to the back of Surrey House (three more 'leads') and Surrey Street, comes into All Saints' Green, near 'Jack's Pit,' a spot bounded now by the residences of prominent medical men.

From this point our course is more clear for some distance, and the boys breathe *more freely, whatever is the case with their seniors, for we now mount the hill, up the Swyne Market, to the Brazen Doors (or, as men would now say, to the 'Lame Dog'). Here we come out, as may be seen from Cunningham's Map, into the open country, and enjoy a charming view across the fields of Lakenham, as we skirt the outside of the old city wall, as far as St Stephen's Gate. Probably the wall was then the western boundary of the parish, the only house outside the walls being the Leper Hospital.*

Turning in at St Stephen's Gate - where the hermit, William Bassett, looks down at our procession from his little room above the gate, - we pass up what is now Coburg Street to where another 'lead' is to be seen, and zigzag again in a somewhat confusing manner to the west of the site of Messrs Caley's works, and round that splendid group of ancient monastic buildings, whose foundations Mr G. E. Hawes has recently been excavating, - the Church and Collegiate buildings of St Mary-in-the-Fields. Through what is now Theatre Square, and a short way down Theatre Street, we proceed up a little passage opposite Chantry Court, and come back into Church Street, at the spot now marked by the last 'lead' that we pass, and so find ourselves once more at the north porch of St Stephen's Church, from which we made our start.

★★★

The boundary of King's Lynn was perambulated in 1829. The *Norfolk Chronicle* tells us that clergymen, wardens and officers of St Margaret's church were involved, together with some 236 boys from the Free School. Each lad was provided with a long white wand for beating upon the boundary. The walk lasted for two hours and included 'duckings' and other happenings associated with such a day of ceremony and merriment. The boundaries were so peculiar on this walk that it required the entry of one property by the front door, and exit via a window. Perhaps 300 people were involved that day, so it must have caused considerable annoyance to the occupiers. Incidentally, the boys present were all treated to a large plum bun and half a pint of beer, at the culmination of their exertions. The elder members of the party dined later in town at the Crown Inn.

Pond, stream and river-duckings were not at all uncommon where they were adjacent to parish perimeters. No doubt such happenings were a lasting means of impressing boundary locations on the parishioners. Sometimes simply an out of the usual occurrence would suffice. In 1595 a New Buckenham man was invited to 'drinke bear out of an hande Bell' at the parish perimeter, to jog his memory of the event in the future.

Living on the boundary line of a parish obviously had its drawbacks. It seems that such an inconvenience as mass intrusion of your premises just had to be put up with. In Chapter Two we shall see that a similar fate befell those living in boundary property, within the parish of St Andrew, Norwich, during 1762. One can also guess that such goings-on greatly added to the overall enjoyment of the day - for the boundary beaters that is!

14

(Left) Two Boundary Plates for St Stephen's parish used in 1804 and 1820. Note the small ram's head, (symbol of a martyr) between the two SS letters in the 1820 plate. These markers (fixed in place in the early 19th century) can still be seen at the rear of the Assembly House, Norwich.

Clergy, officials and choir of St Andrew's, Norwich, processing their bounds along Castle Meadow, in 1957. Note leading boys are carrying 'wands'.

In 1952 the vicar and choirboys of St Andrew's, are beating their boundary 'line' through a newspaper office composing room, then situated in nearby Redwell Street. Note that the boys are beating with 'wands' which have ceremonial tassels attached at their ends for extra effect.

CHAPTER TWO

Beating the Bounds in Georgian Norwich

Georgian Norwich was composed of many parishes, each responsible for control over buildings, pathways, pavements, fire-fighting, crime prevention, civic festivities and many other social or protective measures. The church was the central organisation of any parish and therefore undertook the supervision of many aspects of 17th and 18th century community life.

We can easily forget that living conditions in our city over three centuries ago were very basic. The absence of sanitation, lighting and transport made for dark and dismal journeys through the streets at night, with the ever-present fear of attack by robbers and the like. Some effort was made to keep the peace by the appointment of constables in every parish. Even so, they could never have been more than an inconvenience to felons roaming the streets at night. Norwich was then even more a city of alleyways than it is now. The ease with which law-breakers could vanish into the shadows, would doubtless frustrate those who tried to maintain some semblance of order.

Against this backcloth it becomes very clear that parish responsibilities were varied, involved, and needing formal control. No parish would wish to take on any extra burden of duty that rightly belonged to its neighbours. However, collecting parish rates from more inhabitants would have been appealing. The income from this source went towards the upkeep of the parish and the church and the care of the destitute. Only those considered to be too poor or destitute would escape paying this yearly rate. In order to prevent disputes over exact parish boundaries, it became vitally important for each church to define its own boundary. More than that, it was essential that such boundaries should be brought to the general notice of the population at large. Disputes over encroachments could then be fairly and satisfactorily challenged and settled, with clear and unambiguous authority.

In the absence of readily available detailed maps of the central city parishes, it fell to the churches themselves to define clearly and display the confines of their boundaries. The method adopted involved the fixing up of metal or stone markers, generally at a safe height. The markers at the very least would display the initials of the parish concerned and also the year that the boundary was redefined. Exceptionally, the markers would bear a longer more elaborate legend. (See pages 19 and 48).

The vast majority of plates still extant are of a fairly regular, rectangular shape. The exception to this rule can be found in some of the plates for the parishes of St Peter Hungate, St George Tombland, and St Andrew. Here the shapes are interesting. (See Chapter Three). As these parishes are adjoining, it is likely that a measure of rivalry crept in. These were three

important and influential churches and none would be prepared to be overshadowed by the others. The placing of a marker of one parish next to another of different ownership would be watched very closely indeed. To have anything looking inferior in plate design would be unthinkable. We do not see this individualistic approach to plate shape elsewhere. However, the designs on some others are quite elaborate and well worth study.

Although the majority of boundary plates will be found to be of rather basic design, containing only a date and the parish initials, there are a number remaining that display some clever features. The patron saints adopted by many parishes have definite symbols by which they are instantly recognised. Those parishes that had the craftsmen available to depict them, used such devices within the plate design. There was an important reason for doing this of course. As space available on the average metal plate was limited, the adoption of an irrefutable distinguishing mark certainly added emphasis, style and clarity to the marker. This was especially true where the initials of adjacent parishes were confusingly similar. Using, in addition, a cleverly shaped plate would be seen as an extra mark of enterprise and prestige.

Although most boundary markers were made of metal, there are four very rare stone tablets still surviving. One is to be found on the Coach and Horses public house in Bethel Street (for the year 1710) and another set into the wall on Micawber's Tavern in Pottergate. Both of these tablets bear the details of two parishes. The former carries the initials of St Peter Mancroft and St Giles and the latter those of St Margaret and, again, St Giles, for the year 1772.

Sharing a stone marker must have involved a degree of inter-parish co-operation, and there must have been a good reason for this. Certainly, it would be difficult to tamper with or remove such a boundary marker. Illegal removal of plates did happen, so it would serve everyone's interests to secure those considered vulnerable. A stone set in a wall is safe from theft.

Both the above stone markers are very plain and carry the absolute minimum of legend, simply a date and two sets of parish initials. When looking at the two other surviving stone markers we find one shows a longer description. It contains the details of one parish only (St George Tombland)

and the date places it between the other two already described. The full legend, on an oblong white stone tablet reads, 'The Boundary of St George's Tombland 1748.' This marker can be found on the premises opposite number 7, St Faiths Lane. It is positioned fairly high in a wall and can easily be missed. Owing to erosion over recent years the lettering is not clear. This site formerly marked the boundary shared by St George Tombland with St Peter Parmentergate. A plate for the latter (dated 1827) went missing from near this area some years ago. The marker in the Bridewell Museum (also 1827) is therefore the only one extant. However, they are not one and the same item, as the one now missing was painted blue when last seen in situ by the author. The museum plate has no trace of recent colouring. Hopefully, it may turn up sometime.

The fourth stone boundary marker is situated in St Giles Street by the archway near the Salvation Army Citadel. Again, it needs searching out, especially as it is a broken fragment. It also dates from 1772 and originally denoted the adjacent parish boundaries of St Giles and St Gregory. Only the St Giles portion remains almost complete, the right hand segment. On the left side of the central line (between the 7s) can be seen a very small 'Y' for Gregory, the only visible remnant of the St Gregory initials.

The excitement of discovering this during a painstaking search of that area on a particularly cold and wet day in May 1985 is a happy memory. Reference to the parish of St Giles is the common factor on both the 1772 tablets. Obviously these quite small carved objects would have been produced in a local stonemason's yard, perhaps as apprentice-pieces.

Further evidence of the placing of this stone marker was discovered on an 1869 watercolour of Mortimer's Hotel in St Giles Street by William Frederick Austin. Every feature of the building is drawn with great clarity, including three metal boundary markers. We can recognise the archway as

1869   2007

that of the Salvation Army Citadel. Above the archway are two plates for St Giles (1829 mounted above 1814) and to the left (rather tarnished) on an adjacent building, that for St Gregory (1828). The artist has very kindly also drawn in the rare stone marker, represented as a white oblong about halfway up the left archway vertical support. This tablet looks to be already showing the damage that we can see today; it is broken and, owing to an obscuring fascia-board, only the right hand portion can be viewed. The date of 1772 can be easily deduced from the '772' numerals in view. Note also the vertical groove dividing the two 7s. This was the precise boundary line between the two neighbouring parishes. In such a busy archway it is not difficult to imagine how this rather low and exposed stone marker could have received its damage.

The physical act of marking the boundary of a parish in a public manner was in the best interests of all. To bring emphasis to the event, the church officers, (priest, churchwardens and leading parishioners) would arrange for a complete circuit of the parish to be made. As stated in the previous a complete circuit of the parish to be made. As stated in the previous chapter, it was undertaken during the church season of Rogationtide, between Easter and the Ascension. The boundary limits would therefore be 'walked', amidst general noise and chanting of prayers. This act of tracing the bounds was usually referred to as 'going the bounds', or as a 'perambulation', the latter variously mis-spelt by some less able parish recorders. (See Chapter Three).

Although this picture is of the Boundary Beating party at St Clement's, Ipswich, in 1902, it does show the willow 'wands' (or osiers) being used that day. The choir-boys have theirs lowered on the ground before them.

During the course of such an event the limits of the parish were actually physically 'beaten', often using long willow sticks variously called 'oziers', 'osiers' or 'wands'. The preference for willow seems to stem from a very ancient pagan belief that it possessed mystical properties. Sometimes ordinary boughs and branches were used. It was not uncommon for people themselves to be beaten with the wands at certain boundary points, or occasionally choir boys would be bumped against buildings marking the perimeter. A favourite method involved hanging the lad upside down and bumping his head on the ground. The serious aspect to this physical beating was to draw maximum attention to the actual boundaries and to fix the exact spot that individuals were beaten. They would then remember the location in the future – long after the headache had worn off.

The many churchwardens' account books studied contain fascinating glimpses into the details of 'going the bounds'. Serious as the event was in terms of official parish duty, such a task was not allowed to stand in the way of much merriment. For instance, the people of St Clement visited no less than eleven public houses in 1821, the day they went the bounds. (See Chapter Three). Not surprisingly, the wealthy parishes spent far more on their perambulations than their poorer fellow citizens. Churches such as St Peter Mancroft, St Clement or St George Tombland would regularly spend twenty to thirty pounds, whereas the folk of St Etheldreda laid out only two pounds four and sixpence in 1768. Modest expense, but this was a much poorer parish.

Even a poor parish would treat its boundary ceremonies with due care. The parish of St Benedict finished up one year 'in the red', but still included a perambulation of its boundary. The year, 1854, is an interesting one in that it marks the last parish boundary walk to be commemorated by a marker plate still surviving in place. It can be seen on Messrs A. C. Leigh's in St Benedict Street. A matching plate is in the Bridewell Museum - original site unknown.

The earliest Norwich reference to an actual boundary walk was discovered on a very fragile scrap of paper, and pre-dates the Georgian era, taking us back to the reign of James II. The parish concerned was that of St Andrew in 1686. This piece of paper was in a bundle of documents in the parish archive in the old Norwich Library. It reads, rather quaintly as follows:

This the 29 of June 1686
[Requested?] then of the Church wardons of the P'ish of Saint Androws for
Cakes for the paramaltion Twelle Shillings for say Bounds by me Tho Mollet.

Mr Mollet was indeed promptly paid his twelve shillings, on 9 July. Sadly there are no plates extant to accompany this perambulation record.

The records of this important Norwich parish church reveal the only detailed account of a Georgian perambulation to emerge in the course of research. This circuit of the parish of Saint Andrew, took place on 20 May 1762. It reveals that a total of sixteen markers were placed on various vantage points on that occasion. This account is so fascinating that it warrants full inclusion here. (Underlining retained from the original).

Memorandum – May 20 1762

This Day, The Minister, Parish Officers and Principal Inhabitants of the Parish of St Andrew in the City of Norwich, did make their Common Perambulation of the Circuit of the said Parish, according to the usual Custom heretofore practiced in the Days of Rogations, In manner following; Viz;

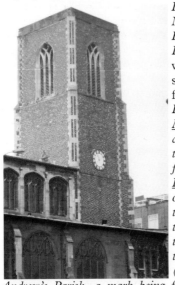

From the said Parish Church, They Proceeded, Northward, to the Bridge called Black Friars Bridge, where they fixed up a Land Mark or Dolle, [from Saxon times the name 'Dale' was given to the annual apportionment of strips of land. The term 'Dolle' derives from this source.] *Eastward of the said Bridge, on the wall of a Building, now a <u>Malthouse</u> or Granary, having the River adjoining on the part of the North:- From thence, down the River, Eastward, where they fixed up a mark or Dolle, on a wall, having the <u>Premises</u> of <u>Matthew Goss Gent</u>, in the Parish of St Peter of Hungate adjoining on the part of the East, and the River, on the North:- From thence, toward the South, a Boy was put over the Wall, who went to the passage leading thro' the <u>Workhouse</u> Yard, thro' the <u>Dutch Church</u>, (which is included within Boundaries of St Andrew's Parish, a mark being fixed up on the East End of the said Dutch Church, Opposite to St Peters of Hungate Church yard;) - from thence, thro' a place called the <u>Green Yard</u>, now in the occupation of the Revd Mr Primatt, thro' Mr Primatt's <u>back yard</u>, into the Common Street, where a Mark was fixed up, having <u>Mr De Hague's</u> house adjoining to the East. - Thence up the Street leading to the <u>Red Well</u>, Southward, turning down a Lane, at the corner of a Publick House, known by the name of the <u>Bell</u>, westward, (at the end of which Lane a mark was fix'd up) thro' the passage, and House now in the occupation of <u>Mr Reeve Baker</u>;- From thence by the common Street, to the <u>Steps</u> going into London Lane, including the Row of houses on the East side of the Street, and the North side of London Lane, thro' the parlour of the house, now in occupation of Mr Kendall, a Quaker; a mark was fix'd up on the said Hou[se facin]g S[aint] Michaels at Plea parish on the East; another mark was fixed up within the said Kendall's yard;- From thence thro' the House, now in occupation of Mr Beckwith Glover; mark fixed up on Beckwiths house thro' his Yard to the Green Yard adjoining to the Castle Ditches, where a mark was fixed up, adjoining to the house of Mr Freeman Carpenter on the East;- From thence down the Castle Ditches, Westward, to the house now in occupation of Mr Cockayne Staymaker: a mark*

23

was fix'd on the house adjoining to the said Cockayne's on the west:- Thro'
Cockayne's house & yard, leading to Cockey Lane, up the back of the Inns,
including the house of the Revd Mr Berney, Stables etc adjoining Mr Page's Work
Shop, west, From thence, across the Street, thro' a Washhouse, belonging to the
house now in the occupation of Mr Richard Hutchinson Silversmith, a mark was
fix'd up on the house adjoining thereto, on the West, - Thro' Mr Girlington's Shop
Barber, into the Cockey Lane, a mark was Fix'd up on the said Girlington's
house, having the house of Mr Brand adjoining to the West, From thence down the
Cockey Lane, turning at the House now in occupation of Mr Rich'd Ward,
Brazier; thro' the Little Cockey Lane, by the wall of Dr Ellis's Garden,
northward. - From thence across the Street called St Andrews lower Street,
Northward down a Yard quite to the River, a mark was fix'd up on the house now
in occupation of Mr Dixon, in the aforesaid Street adjoining to the house of Mr
Barnham on the West: and another at the Bottom of the yard, was fix'd up to the
wall, having the River adjoining the North:- From thence down the River,
Eastward, to Blackfriars Bridge, where a mark was fix'd up, on the house of Mr
Marston Soap Boiler, having the Bridge on the East, and the River on the North
- This Circuit includes the parish of St Andrews in the City of Norwich

> *Wm Claggett; Curate of*
> *Saint Andrews Parish...*
> *May 20 1762......................*

Some observations cannot be resisted after reading this very detailed
perambulation. It is very clear that the official circuiting of the parish
bounds gave absolute and complete licence for those involved to have free
access to all property where necessary. Remember the mention of the
walkers going *through* the house and yard where Mr Cockayne lived. Mr
Reeve, the baker, fared little better when all and sundry tramped through his
home. To live in property on the edge of a parish was obviously an
occupational hazard. Imagine the scene after perhaps up to fifty people had
trudged through your house on a wet and muddy day. Such tenants must
have rejoiced that this was not always an annual event.

It is hardly surprising that so many trades were going on in St Andrew's
parish, always an important location. Remember too, we only have mention
of those conducting their businesses on the boundary line of the parish.
The trades mentioned were bakers, carpenters, silversmiths, glovers,
staymakers, barbers, braziers and, perhaps most bizarre of all, a soap boiler.
In fact, soap boiling was a popular industry in Norwich at this time. The
soap was made, mainly for the textile industry, out of tallow imported from
as far away as Russia. In 1845 the soap boilers of Norwich manufactured
over 1½ million pounds of the product for household as well as industrial
use.

An intriguing feature of the above 1762 perambulation is the actual number of markers fixed up. A total of sixteen were put in place and it can be assumed that such a total would normally be fixed when this parish was circuited. A smaller parish would no doubt require fewer markers, but there may well have been exceptions to this rule, for instance where a small parish was encroached upon by a number of others.

Some lead boundary markers weigh ten pounds each, not an inconsiderable weight. The 1762 perambulation in St Andrew's would have necessitated almost 1½ cwt (c. 76 kilograms) of metal to be carried around on that day in order to fix up sixteen plates. Even if several people were pressed into sharing the load with handcarts, it would still be quite a task – working up a thirst, of course! The method adopted in some parishes was to fix the plates into place some time before the actual boundary beating took place. The entry in Chapter Three under St George Tombland, 1777, is relevant. Apart from avoiding fatigue, it would allow for an almost uninterrupted physical beating of the bounds to take place. As an appealing bonus - longer visits could be made to the inns and hostelries en route!

The prime function of parish boundary markers was to show unambiguously where one parish ended and another began. This system took care of most disputes arising over exact boundaries. However, there were exceptions. One such incident concerned a dispute, which arose over the death of a person at an address in Pottergate. In Georgian times this long street formed part of the border of no less than six parishes. Such complexity led to the confusion.

The crux of the matter was that no one could agree which parish the bedroom actually belonged to. Owing to its rather strange construction, the room in question projected into the building structure of the adjoining house. Until the correct parish could be determined, the body had to remain exactly where it was. The conjecture was ultimately resolved and the body removed.

The site of this controversy can still be visited in Pottergate where, mounted high on the building above number 10, (adjacent to Barney's Courtyard), can be seen the boundary marker for St John Maddermarket, dated 1829. By a bizarre twist of fate, only a few years ago this building housed a cosmetic establishment called The Body Shop.

Whilst discussing Pottergate, another site of interest and importance can be mentioned. At its furthest end where it joins Cow Hill and Ten Bell Lane, will be found a public house called Micawber's Tavern. Below a first floor window

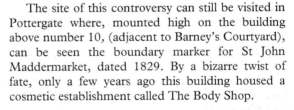

facing onto Pottergate Street can be seen a small stone tablet bearing the date 1772. A careful inspection will reveal that it contains the initials of two parishes, those of St Margaret and St Giles. As mentioned earlier, stone markers are now very rare indeed. Do go and see this one.

On the subject of St Giles' parish boundaries, the following tale is worth recounting. In 1814, during the beating of the bounds, a rather special event had to be included because part of the boundary passed through what we know as Chapelfield Gardens. In 1814 this area was known as Chappley Fields.

The complication arose because at this time it was the city reservoir. One of the party of 'beaters' agreed to swim across the lake to observe the exact line of the boundary. We do not know if the intrepid swimmer actually demanded danger money, but we are told he was rewarded by the not insignificant payment of half a crown. The area flooded (from 1792 until 1854) is said to have been approximately 90 yards long by 50 yards wide, slightly smaller than a football pitch.

Here is yet another example of the very serious way in which boundary beating was observed and conducted. Was there any evidence of the boundary of St Giles church passing through Chapelfield Park to corroborate this interesting story? Sure enough, going back to the OS map of the area was revealing.

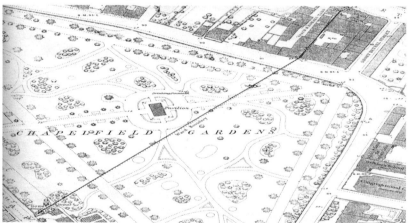

Reproduced from the 1884 Ordnance Survey Map with permission, Crown copyright

The Ordnance Survey map of 1884, (even though some seventy years later than 1814) still shows clearly the ward boundary 'line' taking its diagonal route through the area mentioned. The actual boundary line dissected the park from a point roughly opposite Little (Short) Bethel Street, straight across its width ending by an extant city wall tower on Chapelfield

Road. It did not become the laid out park we know and love today until 1877. The parish of St Stephen is to the right of the line, and that of St Giles (where this slight digression started) above and left of the line as viewed in the map.

[On a personal note, I well remember the same rewarding coin (half a crown) being the rate for the job when singing as a choirboy for weddings in the 1950s, at St James' church in Pockthorpe, Norwich. It seemed a princely sum to me then, so in 1814 one can imagine no shortage of volunteers willing to take on this swim.]

Although boundary beating in Norwich usually only involved the redefining of parish borders, we know that the boundaries of the whole City were beaten in 1803. On this occasion the Mayor, two Sheriffs, other City officials and some citizens, rode the boundary of the City on horseback. Bands were playing and colours flying as the party moved off from Conesford Gate. The circuit was made by way of Trowse, Lakenham, Harford Bridge, Eaton, Earlham, Hellesdon, Mile Cross, Catton, across Mousehold to Thorpe Hamlet. From there down to Bishop Bridge and finally back to the cross in the Market Place. After three hearty cheers were observed, the bands played 'God Save the King'.

In the evening, following true perambulation tradition, the Mayor dined with a large gathering at the King's Head, which stood on what we today call Gentleman's Walk, where it joins Davey Place. Only ten years after this big civic celebration the King's Head was put up for sale and the entrepreneurial (not to mention controversial) Alderman Jonathan Davey bought it and demolished the building. He opened up the site as a pedestrian shopping area, linking it through to the Back of the Inns.

CHAPTER THREE

Official Parish Record Books
Extracts & Observations 1678-1854

This chapter presents perambulation details that mainly correspond with the years for which boundary plates are still extant. Some of the ledger entries are rather brief. Often only the amount spent is quoted. Nevertheless, in a few cases, detailed accounts of where the perambulation parties took their refreshments have come to light. Not only is this interesting in itself, but it also indirectly plots the boundary via the hostelries visited. Even if the boundary was beaten infrequently, such a very public event served to bond the local parish community.

It will be seen in the account book entries that drinking beer was an important feature of the day's outing. Does this mean that these events were for men only? We know that youngsters were sometimes in attendance because they were 'bumped' on the boundary, from time to time along the way. Children also occasionally had their own refreshments provided and paid for. There is never any direct mention of women being present amongst the boundary walkers. However, ladies of the parish quite often provided food and drink at certain lodgings along the way.

Large amounts of money were spent on some occasions and, where this was anticipated, the gentlemen taking dinner were expected to pay for their meals. It has been said that expenses could only be claimed every three years. None of the research for this book supports this view. Copious quantities of beer flowed at some perambulations and enormous numbers of cakes were sometimes consumed. At one event 18 dozen cakes (216) were eaten by children on their own, but unfortunately we do not know how many hungry youngsters made this trip. It is quite likely that these cakes were the only sustenance eaten that day. Can we hear the parents imploring their little mites to get down to the church for some free buns?

Notes follow the various account book entries (together with marker illustrations where possible) to explain more about the actual event. Observations are also included which shed light on some interesting people and the places where they lived.

Parish of St Benedict
Churchwardens' account book for 1854/55

Although no direct reference is made to the perambulation in 1854, we know that they did mark the occasion because plates are still extant for that year. As stated elsewhere, this particular year is important because it was the last year in which any Norwich parish beat its bounds *and* left us a plate in situ as evidence. From the accounts for years leading up to this date, it is very clear that there was not much spare funding to support any special event. Easter 1852 was the last time the accounts show any profit was made, and this a paltry 4s.7½d. The only marker plate still in position within the parish can be seen mounted on Messrs A.C. Leigh's premises in St Benedict Street.

Parish of St Clement
Churchwardens' Rate Book 1779 - 1820
(Regrettably, no plates exist for 1788)

April 28th 1788. *At a Parish Meeting held this Day at the Vestry it was unanimously agreed to go the Bounds of this Parish to Morrow being Tuesday 29th April 1788, the Parishioners to meet at the Vestry at 10 o'clock in the forenoon and from thence proceed round the Parish.*

April 29 *Going the Bounds of the Parish.*	
Dinner and Wine at the Bull	*£4. 4. 4*
Do. 18 doz cakes for the children	*18. 0*
July 21 Beer at going the Bounds to Mr Hogg	*8. 0*
Sept 17 Beer at going the Bounds to Mr Haylett	*5. 0*
Sept 24 Beer at going the Bounds to Mr Beevis	*9. 0*

total expense £6. 4. 4

Not much in the way of detail for this event. Unfortunately we have no plates surviving for this year either. The July and September dates for beer payments indicate that the church did not pay its bills very promptly. The two following extracts, however, give us much more information, and a real flavour of the events and their social importance.

St Clement, 1809
Tudor rose and anchor. Number 19 Colegate. St Clement was persecuted then drowned at sea with an anchor about his neck. This device later became adopted as a universal symbol of steadfast hope.

Churchwardens' Rate Book 1779 - 1820
May 1st 1809, *at a Vestry meeting held this day it was unanimously agreed to go the Bounds of the Parish of St Clements on the 8th of May 1809*
Thomas Norman & Jos. Payne Church Wardens

29

May 8th *For going the bounds of the Parish*

Dinner, Wine and Porter at Mr Atkins's	*£12. 11. 8*
Cushen for shewing the Bounds	*2. 6*
Mr Branch, for Cakes for the Children	*£1. 1. 0*
Clerk and Sexton Parish Meeting	*2. 0*
Wands and Boughs	*2. 6*
For Ringing the Bells	*7. 6*
Mrs Clabburn for Oranges etc	*13. 0*
Beer at different houses	*£2. 1. 0*
Do for the Ringers and Plumbers	*6. 6*
total expenses £17. 7. 8	

Yet another charming glimpse into our city's past can be found in the accounts for this boundary walk. Six shillings and sixpence was allowed to the bell-ringers for their beer money. We do not know where it was spent. A further seven shillings and sixpence was paid to the ringers for pealing the bells. This was the method used to call the parishioners together at the church porch, and thereby proclaim a start to the festivities.

Bell-ringing in Norwich was far more prevalent during this time than it is now, the prime reason being the mass removal of bells from unsafe redundant church towers during recent decades. Many account books have entries of fees paid to bell-ringers on various festive occasions. The monarch's birthday, and national days of thanksgiving were often marked in this fashion. Nelson's famous victory at Trafalgar in 1805 was so proclaimed. With his local origins this was fitting and hardly surprising.

It is good to be able to say that the bells of four city churches (St Giles, St Peter Mancroft, St George Colegate and St Michael & All Angels) do still regularly peal across our historic rooftops. Long may this be so.

Surprisingly, there is no mention of visits to alehouses in the above 1809 details. One imagines that the dinner at Mr Atkins's house must have been quite lavish. It absorbed about two thirds of the total outlay for the event. The reference to Mr Cushen 'shewing the Bounds' is of interest. He was very likely to have been one of the parish elders. This would have been his chance to earn a few shillings and some kudos in pointing out where the boundary line of the parish lay. Some boundaries were quite difficult to follow accurately. It made sense to have someone knowledgeable showing the way.

The children got their chance to have a treat as usual. There is no reference to the manner of this perambulation, so we do not know if any children were 'bumped' along the way. Probably they were, or lightly beaten with the wands, at certain places round the parish. The thought of boys being beaten is not one we are comfortable with today but no references to hurtful outcomes in this part of the ceremony have been found. Feeding the children with nice plump cakes could also have been part and parcel of impressing the overall event on their memories.

Liquid refreshment was apparently taken at a number of private houses along the way. Perhaps it was a strong home-brew. Anyway we see that the thirsty bell-ringers were up the front as usual. Very dusty up those church towers! The reference to 'Plumbers' makes one wonder whether they were responsible for casting the lead plates, two of which, for this very year, can still be found in Colegate. (See page 34 and 35 and Appendix B).

Church Wardens' Rate Book 1821 – 1861

May 11th 1821 *At a Vestry Meeting held this day it was unanimously agreed to Perambulate the Bounds of the Parish on Monday the 28th Day of May and following Days next ensuing and it is also agreed that a Dinner be provided at the Bull and that each Gentleman who intends Dining to pay the sum of Four Shillings.*

28 May

Bellman for giving notice to out Layers	2. 00
Stewardson & Bokenham	2. 00
Black Boys Culyer for Beer	5. 01
Anchor Bagshaw	14. 06
Jack of Newbury Bennet	12. 06
Red Lion Redrum	10. 00
Elm Harrison	12. 04
Whale Bone Sexton	19. 00
True Briton Brighton	8. 00
Windmill	12. 02
Swann	19. 00
Pine Apple	14. 00
Goose for cakes	10. 00
Watson ditto	11. 00
Culyer ditto	£1. 00. 00
Manning ditto	£1. 09. 02
Paid Bales Ringing and Engine	£1. 03. 06
Ringers allowance at the Bull	2. 06
Curson 2nd Day	1. 06
Gay for Oscer [see below]	12. 00
Desert £1. 11. 6 Ices 7/6	£1. 19. 00
Servants at the Bull	10. 00
Duckell Bill £26. 12. 6 by 30 4/- each £6	£20. 12. 06
Perambulating the Boundary	£35. 2. 7

This is an amazingly detailed account of what must have been an epic event. It was anticipated by the Vestry meeting that the total journey might take more than one day, and so it proved. One imagines that this was not uncommon. Even so, it is the only reference found that was so categorical about the anticipated duration of the perambulation. Perhaps it was the practice in some parishes to have a really sumptuous perambulation from time to time. It is not surprising that this one was spread over two days when visits were made to no less than 11 public houses.

What is really staggering is the amount of ale drunk. It is possible to arrive at an estimated consumption figure, based on the known cost (£1.0.8d) of 62 quarts of beer in the 1786 accounts for St Etheldreda's church. Therefore, at 2d per pint, the expense of £6.9.1d for beer suggests a likely total of 775 pints, about 70 pints per pub. It is almost impossible to believe, but doubtless most of the very merry band slept well the first night - if not the second, also. Is it still possible to trace the 1821 pub-crawl?

The Black Boys public house is still with us in Colegate, but known these days as The Merchants of Colegate. A boundary plate commemorating this very perambulation in 1821, can still be found mounted on the front of the building. It is the top-most of the three, partially obscured by a drainpipe.

It is difficult now to find precise locations for some of the other alehouses visited. The only one that can be placed for certain is the Jack of Newbury that was still using this name during the 1960s. It is now trading as a restaurant called The Torero and stands directly opposite the junction of Colegate with Magdalen Street, although, strictly speaking, it is on Fye Bridge Street. Looking at the frontage of this building one can see that it was once a public house; there has been no drastic remodelling. The original name of Jack of Newbury is a reference to John Winchcome of Newbury (1465-1519). He was a very wealthy cloth merchant.

The Red Lion is a real problem, as there were no fewer than four alehouses so called within the neighbourhood. Probably the only one strictly within the parish, is the building at number 19 Magdalen Street. This rather small property is now trading as Presence after undergoing drastic refurbishment during late 2005. This address is right on the border of the parish, which only just squeezes in number 21 next door. A parish boundary plate for the very year in question (1821) can be seen mounted high up on the adjoining shop frontage, used by Messrs Looses until 2005.

The Bull Inn is a little easier to deal with as it was to be found at number 5 Magdalen Street. This was a very old coaching house from possibly the early seventeenth century. It was lately the premises of the Marie Curie charity shop. Its double width frontage makes it easy to imagine its former heyday. No doubt it put on a good spread for the thirty diners from the church opposite.

The entry 'Bellman giving notice to out Layers', no doubt infers that the bellman's stentorian call was heard about the parish, alerting those involved that they were needed at the church. Here was an opportunity for this regular employee, who sang out the hours during the night, to earn a couple of extra shillings.

The main church bells were pealed in order to call the general throng of supporters to the church at the designated hour. Prayers would be said for a general blessing of the event before the procession moved off. Litanies to the Almighty were also sung during the perambulation of the bounds. The money paid to 'Bales Ringing and Engine' indicates that it was almost certain that Mr Bales, apart from organising the church bell-ringers also engaged the parish fire appliance to play its part in the colourful scene.

The almost illegible entry in the churchwarden's rate book 'Gay for Oscer', tells us that Mr Gay was charged with the provision of osiers, which is an alternative word (and spelling) used then to describe the willow wands. As we know, these served for pointing out, (and beating upon) the parish boundary points. The entry at the end of the account refers to the cost of the dinner at The Bull, for which it was agreed that the gentlemen would contribute four shillings each, to help defray the overall cost. This explains what is meant by the wording 'by 30 4/- each £6.' The ten shillings paid to the servants was no doubt for waiting at table. As with the 1809 perambulation, there are still boundary plates extant for 1821 to study. (See Appendix B).

Parish of St Etheldreda
In the "Disbursements" of Thomas Burrell and Francis Platt, (Churchwardens) for Easter 1786-1787, we find the following:-

1786
25 May Expences on going the Bounds of the Parish.

Baker Smith for Victuals etc	*12. 4*
ditto for Drinks etc as pr Bill	*19. 6*
Mr Partridge as pr Bill	
62 Qrs Beer for the parish followers	*£1. 00. 8*

Victuals for the same	9. 2
Mr Pallant for Beer as per Bill	5. 0
Mr Platt for cakes etc	5. 0
Mr Foster for Leads and Truble	

Total expenses £3. 11. 8

The incomplete entry regarding Mr Foster's 'Truble' raised the question of whether he had made the plates, especially as the term 'Leads' was used, without doubt referring to the boundary markers. We know that the metal plates used in Norwich were of two types: lead, in the earlier examples, and later in cast iron. It is difficult to be categorical about the transition from one metal to the other. A rough guide would suggest that lead was phased out about 1815 when perhaps it became too expensive. Of course, an advantage of using lead would have been the prospect of easily melting down old plates for re-use. This may well explain significant gaps in sequential year-dates, as regards extant plates. Recycling is not a new idea. Naturally, it is not hard to guess how the plates were manufactured in either of the metals, as both would have involved forming in a mould. It would be nice to think that our Mr Foster was a member of the 'cast' in this parish. The design element in plates does not vary a great deal within a parish, even over a number of years. This could mean that the same craftsman or workshop foundry was regularly entrusted with the work. Because of the serious nature of the boundary-marking ritual, a church authority would never seek the manufacture of its individualistic plates in another parish if it could be avoided. Also there would be a desire for the final dressed quality of the plates to be utterly dependable. This might not be achieved by continually changing craftsmen. Some of the lettering and design components were obviously 'turned-in' for succeeding years, and these would be more easily available if stored in one place. Would a later account book entry help unravel the mystery of the incomplete expenses entry? Sure enough, almost a year later, we find:

17 March 1787
> *Mr Charles Foster, paid his bill. £2. 1s.4½d*

Assuming that this is the same gentleman, perhaps we can say that the boundary plates for 1786 were at least included within the sum mentioned above. A few pages further on there appears another entry of interest:

14 March 1789
> *To Mr Foster, Glazier 8s. 8½d*

Are all three references to one and the same person? If so, it would appear that our Mr Foster was the parish glazier and, if this was the case, he would be more than able to handle the production of the plates. Working with lead would be part of the trade of a glazier, especially if called upon to repair portions of stained glass in the church windows. They would be set into strips of cast lead then, as indeed they are now.

One of the thrills of unearthing historical information lies in relating it to an item still in existence today. Happily, two boundary plates, more than likely made by our Mr Charles Foster, can be found today in King Street. One is mounted on the wall of number 168, and the other on the Music House opposite. Both plates are positioned so as to make inspection of them very easy. This far end of King Street is a fair step out of central Norwich, but the walk is worth while to see the only plates known to exist for this church. So perhaps, at least in this parish, the mystery of the plate maker is solved. Mr Foster is our man.

Parish of St George, Tombland
In the accounts for Easter 1777 to Easter 1778 we find the following entries:-

1777
May 2nd Allow'd Baltis for going the Bounds of the parish and fixing the Number of Leads for that purpose   1. 6d

1778
Paid Wm Trowers Bill for the Feast at his House on the 15 May 1777, the day of Perambulation   10. 10. 00
Paid Baltis for Wands of G. Chamberlain same day   2. 00

This account is very interesting as it does contain clear evidence that sometimes the boundary markers would be in place *before* the merry band set off. Although the St Andrew 1762 perambulation details clearly tell us that the markers were put in place actually *during* the circuit of the parish; this may not have always been the case.

We know that the perambulation took place on 15 May in 1777 so it looks certain that, at least on that occasion, the boundary markers had been secured in place almost two weeks earlier. Mr Baltis was found to be the Parish Clerk and, according to the account book for 1778, he also arranged for the provision of the willow wands used to beat the boundaries the previous year. Incidentally, his own signature can be found on an adjoining page in the ledger for 1777, and it reads 'William Balltis'.

There are other entries in parish accounts, which state that ordinary branches from sapling trees were used. Once again, it looks as though a few people had to wait several months to get their bills settled. It is still possible to find three boundary plates for the year 1777. It is likely that each one is exactly where William Balltis fixed it over two centuries ago. The sites to visit in order to see the 1777 plates will be found detailed in the Index, at Appendix B.

Parish of St Gregory
Churchwardens' Accounts for 1828 - 1829

1828

Allowance Beer when going bounds of the parish		*£8.16. 5*
Bill at Vine Tavern on going bounds of the parish		*£1. 6. 6*
Staffs Bill for cakes,	*ditto*	*10. 0*
Hilling's	*ditto*	*10. 0*
Simpson's	*ditto*	*10. 0*
Welton's	*ditto*	*10. 0*
Hovell for Oziers		*7. 6*
Total expences £12. 9/5d		

This is the account for the perambulation in Rogationtide 1828. Interestingly, we have plates for this parish for 1828 *and* 1829. They can be seen in Westwick Street and St Giles Street respectively. It was unusual for parish bounds to be beaten in successive years. However, one always had to keep an eye on the neighbours. Other account books for this parish contained some rather wonderful examples of copperplate writing. The title page for the year 1771 is a real feast of beauty. An appropriate fee of twelve shillings was paid to a Mr Satchy, for his considerable skill.

St John Timberhill, 1826.
The central design feature is a mound of overlapping leaves (a 'timber hill').
18 Golden Ball Street, opposite The Woolpack.

1826
[Scribbled in the margin of the accounts is the following:]
Perambulation 1826 The Dinner at the Star & Crown

Sadly, no mention of the expense or anything else. We do however still have five plates extant for this year. The Star & Crown was located on Timberhill.

The picture below sheds an interesting light on this area of Norwich. It has often been published as an '18th century drawing' of the view near the

Woolpack public house, on Golden Ball Street. I have to declare it to be a fake. I had the thought that I had seen something like it before somewhere but as a photograph, and eventually tracked down the picture to page 81 of 'Norwich Old and New' by Michael Shaw (EP Publishing 1974). The photograph was taken c. 1900, and the window (above, top left) supposedly thrown open in perhaps 1780, was still open in the 1900 photograph!

However, if this drawing is indeed based on the photograph of 1900, with figures added and some windows altered, it does have some merit. The photograph in the book had been cropped so as to lose most of the building on the left, but the artist has included what are obviously three boundary plates in his drawing. If these plates were indeed on the negative of the 1900 photograph, it is possible to identify not only the location of the pictured buildings, but also the parishes to which the markers belonged.

On the face of it, the two rectangular plates (All Saints) are in the correct place, but the oval item seems to be on the wrong side of the road, as it belongs to St John Timberhill. However, scrutiny of the parish map interestingly revealed that St John's parish did indeed own a small portion of land that was cut into the All Saints parish at this very spot. Here is further evidence of how vital a plate could be in emphasizing a parish boundary, especially where it would seem to contradict logic.

It can therefore be stated with certainty that the view above is not of Golden Ball Street but of a prospect looking down Westlegate from All Saints Green. The rectangular boundary plates read ASP 1712 and PAS 1825 both being for All Saints Parish, and the oval marker is incorrectly drawn as PUSA 1826. In fact the initials should state SJTH i.e. St John

Timberhill, and this is a year we have information about. In fact there are two plates of this type still extant around that parish at 18 Golden Ball Street and 37 All Saints Green. Sadly the All Saints parish plates pictured have vanished. However, it is possible to say with some certainty that Mr Read, whose 1934/35 findings are to be found at Appendix A, actually logged these plates under 'Westlegate Gable end of 7 (3)' So the enigma of the fake picture is solved.

Parish of St Julian

1706
At ye Perambulation   £3. 4. 8d
1709
ffor the Perambulation   £3. 15. 6d
1711
Spent at ye Perambulation   £3. 0. 4d
1726
Expences at the Perambulation   £4. 19/8d
1733
To charges at ye Preamblation   £4. 3/6d
1740
Paid at the Peramalation   £2. 18/6d
1753
Pd at the Preambelation &c   £4. 13/6d

The above details, with their rather quaint spellings, are very sparse and tell us nothing of those taking part on those boundary walks. From the fact that what appear to be small outlays of expense were, on some occasions, up to sixty per cent of that year's outgoings, it will be seen just how important it was to observe boundary beating. St Julian was certainly one of the poorer parishes. There are no marker plates still in existence for the dates mentioned above, but there are four plates for later years, to be found at the far end of King Street. (See Appendix B for details).

Parish of St Laurence, 1806 *A grid-iron.* On wall in Westwick Street, Charing Cross end, underneath overhanging ivy. St Laurence was martyred on a grid-iron, which grisly implement is depicted on the plate.

Sadly, only plates for 1806 survive. It would have been nice to have examples for the following entries.

1678

Payd on a perambulation	*£2. 0. 0*
For beer and tobacco after dinner	*10. 0*
For cakes and beer for the boys	*8. 8*

1696

For bread and beer at the perambulation
being kept at the 2 Brewers in St. Laurence,
meat and attendance   *£4. 6. 6*

The reference to the provision of tobacco is the only one discovered anywhere. The mention of beer for the boys would seem to suggest that they believed in training the youngsters early in the ways of enjoying the boundary celebrations.

Parish of St Mary, Coslany
This plate dated 1792 is the oldest item known extant for this parish. It is part of the archive at the Bridewell Museum. Its original site is not known.

1679

Payd to John Mann for the perambulation	*£2. 7. 0*
Paid at the Unicorn for beef and mutton.....	*£1. 1. 3*
For making 2 pies and flour............................	*3. 0*
To Stephen Cocks for bread and cake...........	*15. 0*
Total expences £4. 6. 3	

Not much can be added to these sparse details apart from noting that The Unicorn stood in Coslany Street, now part of Oak Street, opposite the opening into St Mary's Plain. A Unicorn Yard sign has disappeared recently. Unfortunately, no 1679 markers are extant. However, others are noted at Appendix B.

Parish of St Peter Hungate
1742

At a Parish Meeting upon going the Bounds of the parish on Monday the 14th day of June 1742.
Ben Jos: Ellis, Minister
Mattw Goss Jos Cushon   Churchwardens.
pd at ye preambleation   £2. 4. 0½d
pd Mr Paston for Bound Marks and painting   8/6d

1776/1777
John Day and Martyn Williment church wardens
May 15th Paid for Cakes & Beer going the
Bounds of the Parish   *8/-*
Paid at The Preambalation   *£2. 19. 00*

1814
Elisha DeHague and William Kidd church wardens
Friday June 24 going Bounds
of the Parish   *17/-*

An interesting feature of the 1742 boundary beating is the reference to Mr Paston providing and painting the markers. Only one plate survives and this is in the Bridewell Museum (see illustration above). Having inspected it, there is no trace of any paint on it. The reverse is stamped 'VI'. Of course, it is more than likely that the original paint was applied as a finishing touch to enhance the appearance of a rather drab lead plate. It may also have served as a weatherproof coating.

When browsing through these old record books, much valuable time was often diverted by the delight of finding reference to a person or an event, that was in some way significant elsewhere. Here in the records of this church, for the year 1814, we discover that one Elisha DeHague (or Dehague) was a churchwarden. You may remember that the St Andrew perambulation (1762) described in Chapter Two in such detail, mentioned that a marker was fixed up in Princes Street (referred to then as 'the Common Street') 'with the house of Mr De Hague adjoining to the east'.

However, before going any further, two gentlemen bearing the same name must be distinguished. Elisha De Hague the elder, was born in the parish of St Michael, Coslany, in 1717. In an illustrious civic career he was appointed Speaker of the City Common Council, in 1754. He rose to become Town Clerk in 1774 and held this office, together with that of Norwich Postmaster, until his death on 11 July 1792, aged 74.

Here, then, we have a direct reference to this gentleman who was a leading member of St Peter Hungate church, quite apart from being the holder of a significant civic office. He would be very well known to the people of St Andrew in the adjacent parish, so important in fact that he received a direct mention in the record book of that other parish.

In 1792, his son, also Elisha De Hague (b.1754), was appointed Town Clerk to succeed his father. In 1783 he was known to be living in Elm Hill, which is but a stone's throw from the family home in Princes Street. He died in November 1826 aged 72. His impressive tomb can be found in the churchyard of St Augustine, on the south prospect adjacent to the porch entrance.

Anther notable mentioned in the St Peter Hungate books and also mentioned in the St Andrew 1762 boundary circuit was Matthew Goss, who was a cloth dyer living near Elm Hill and churchwarden in 1742 detailed above. He also generously gave the mayoral gold chain and medallion to the City. However he was himself never mayor. He died in 1779. Mr Reeve the baker gets a mention and paid £1. 3. 4d annual rent to St Peter Hungate church in 1744. There was also mention in 1762 of the property of Dr Ellis, the former Minister of St Peter Hungate, who left the living in that parish on 8 October 1754 and who, in 1762, was still living in the neighbourhood.

Other account book entries for this church are worthy of mention:

15 March 1768 - 3 elm trees planted sw cnr of churchyard by Joseph Bean - at own [his] expence.
25 December 1818 tolling the bell for Death of the Queen ... the sum of 10/-
24 August 1857. An elm tree planted on 3 April 1826 was mutilated by persons unknown - not merely trimmed but deprived of all its branches. Efforts to determine who was responsible have proved to be fruitless.

Even though this famous thoroughfare has had a splendidly prominent plane tree for many years now, references to elm trees in the vicinity of Elm Hill are most appropriate. Wanton vandalism is obviously nothing new.

The 'tolling the bell' would be an act of respect for the passing of Queen Charlotte, consort to King George III, who died at Kew, on Tuesday 17 November, 1818

The name of this very interesting church and parish has, I believe, nothing at all to do with 'hanging' or 'hung' gates. In fact, it is believed that the strange title derives from a corruption of Hound Gate. There apparently was a custom in centuries past of blessing the hounds taking part in local hunts. Here, it is said, the hounds were brought to be blessed at the church gates. This may or may not be so, but an old map of the district dated 1789, does show a dog pound just below the churchyard on Elm Hill. Is this the 'hound' connection?

Parish of St Peter Mancroft, 1813 plain (left) & 1827 with two crossed keys. Coach and Horses public house, Bethel Street. The keys are in fact wrongly depicted. The 'wards' (those projections that turn the lock mechanism) are incorrectly turned inwards. Crossed keys are the symbol of Saint Peter who looks after the gates of heaven.

The accounts of Thomas Cruso, churchwarden:

1813

16 May Boundary Expenses   £24. 2. 6d

In the Churchwardens' accounts for the above year it is stated that '... *the churchwardeans, accompanied by the Rev. Chapman and a great number of the inhabitants, perambulated the boundaries of the parish, and, afterwards dined together at Mrs. Backs'*. On this circuit of the parish bounds several new lead markers were put up, and, in addition, a stone marker was erected on the Castle ditches. Only two lead markers exist today for this date. It is particularly sad that the stone boundary mark cannot be found. In passing, it appeared that a Mr Cruso, Wine Merchant, was paid £20. 2. 4d by the church, during the 1813/14 accounting year.

The accounts of churchwardens Peter Day and William Geary, Easter 1827-1828:-

1827

Thursday 17th May 1827. Notice having been given on Sunday last requiring the Parishioners to meet at the Vestry this day at 12 o'clock precisely to take into consideration the propriety of going the Parish Bounds and to determine in what manner the expenses usually attending the occasion should be defrayed. And also to consider other Parish Affairs -

It was at such Meeting unanimously resolved That the Parish Bounds should be taken on Thursday next at ten o'clock in the forenoon, and that a Dinner be provided for the Parishioners at 7/6 each, and the residue of the expence of taking the Bounds should be borne and paid by the Parishioners out of the Church Rate, for the ensuing year -

The total cost of the perambulation was £32. 18. 10d

We do not have any details of where the perambulation team took their refreshments in 1827. However, we do know that prankish mischief, as usual, was afoot. If imprinting the memory was important on Thursday 17 May 1827, we know someone who would be able to recall the event for several years.

It is certain that the Revd John Bowman of St Peter Mancroft remembered his part in the ceremonial goings-on. A member of the boundary walking party drew a bucket of water from the pump then sited on Hay Hill, and completely soaked the poor man. He later 'dried out' at the Angel Inn. The Arcade entrance on Gentleman's Walk now roughly occupies this site. Incidentally, the Angel was a famous and very ancient building, dating back at least to Elizabethan times. It saw its fair share of amazing displays, including an elephant (1685) 'monsters', freaks, fat women, giants, wax works, a 'hairy childe' and dancing horses. In 1825 a Mon. du Pain (sic) dipped his naked feet into molten lead. So, two years later, the sight of the soaked Revd Bowman may not have merited a second glance!

Getting a good soaking featured in many a perambulation in other parishes too. The following is typical. The revellers from St John de Sepulchre parish in 1820 finished their walk at the Richmond Hill Tavern, on Ber Street. Just as they all assembled outside, a prankster totally drenched everyone with water from an upstairs window. It got worse. The water went into the ale and diluted it. Many must have thought that this was taking practical joking just a bit too far. Interestingly, all the boys were given their own commemorative beer mugs for this event. Sadly, no plates exist.

As perambulation expenses go, the St Peter Mancroft 1827 event cost a princely sum. We have seen earlier that the parish followers of St Clement ran up a bill of over £35 in 1821. We may safely assume that the St Peter Mancroft event must have involved plentiful liquid refreshment stops along the way. Five plates for this year still survive. (See Appendix B)

As stated elsewhere, this parish, together with its neighbour, St Giles, has the oldest surviving marker extant in Norwich. The two parishes decided to share a marker in 1710. The fact that it is in stone, is the oldest and that it is

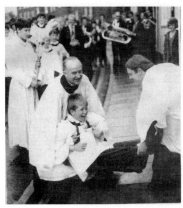

shared, makes this tablet, on the Coach and Horses, Bethel Street, a very important one in Norwich. In 1994, choirboys of St Peter Mancroft were bumped here, as pictured left. Bell-ringing is still regularly undertaken at this magnificent church and would certainly have played its part in boundary ceremonies. However, the local populace have not always appreciated the delights of bell-pealing from this particular church tower. I have seen the following verse (probably 18th century) ascribed to a parishioner of St Peter Mancroft who felt moved to write:

Ye rascally ringers - inveterate foes,
Disturbers of those who are fond of repose,
I wish for the peace and quiet of these lands,
That ye had round your necks
What ye Pull with your hands!

APPENDIX A

The Boundary Marker Survey November 1934-March 1935
J. E. Read

I have said earlier how very indebted we are to Mr Joseph Read, who undertook the last city parish boundary marker survey. As a private individual like myself, he must have consumed many hours of his free time on this task. No doubt we felt the same excitement pursuing this absorbing subject.

He and I must have turned the same pages in those fascinating parish account books. Several hours of careful reading sometimes only yielded a few words of immediate use. Even more frustrating was finding no trace of the entry on which so much was thought to hang. A rather similar feeling would be the despair in finding that a building, annotated in 1934 as displaying marker plates, was still standing, but that only the screw-holes for fixing the plates in position now remained. Finding no building at all seemed even worse of course.

I feel I can do no more to thank Mr Read than to present his largely unpublished findings here in this section of my book. I am proud to pay him this belated tribute for his public-minded interest. The one drawback to the 1934 survey is that it did not identify which parish had plates displayed at the locations detailed. If you know the boundaries well, it can, with some difficulty, be worked out. In my following 2007 survey (Appendix B) I seek to clarify the situation by listing the parish identities at the various locations. If nothing else is achieved, it will make the task of any succeeding enthusiast much easier.

Where I have felt it necessary, the actual entry has been translated from the author's original abbreviated style. My hope is that a fuller explanation will allow the information to be more easily understood, and that the sites listed may be more readily identifiable.

[N.B. The first digit refers to the actual quantity of markers at the location, the second is the address]

1   All Saints Green 37
1   St Andrew's Street 16
2   St Andrew's Hall on East End Buttresses
1   Ber Street 14
4   Bull Close Road, Pipe Burner's Yard - back (2) front (2)
3   Barrack Street 87
7   Bethel Street Coach & Horses (5) 52, 54
2   Bethel Street back of 52, 54

1	Bedford Street - School Lane
1	Bishopgate - Boundary Wall of Bishop's Garden
3	Charing Cross 12,13,15
1	Coburg Street – Caley's Factory corner
6	Cowgate 128 (2) 120 (2) Ruins of Whitefriars Bridge (2)
8	Colegate - Martineau Hall (1) 19 (2) 50 (4) 53 (1)
3	Colegate Blackboys P H (3)
6	Calvert Street 36 (3) Doughty's Hospital (2) Gable 57 (1)
7	Church Street East side (4) West side (3)
1	Duke Street 37
1	Exchange Street next to Corn Hall
4	Elm Hill 39 (2) 2 Buttresses Blackfriars Hall (2)
3	ditto Towler's Court entrance
3	Fishergate - Thoroughfare Yard 10 (3)
2	Farmer's Avenue Plough Inn
1	Golden Dog Lane 15
2	Golden Ball Street 18 (1) 20 (1)
1	Grapes Hill - top left side
1	Hungate Museum
8	King Street 190 (2) 166 (3) Music House (3)
1	Orford Hill 9
5	Pitt Street Gable end 53 (3) and 25 (2)
9	Princes Street 2-4 (4) 16 (3) Haldenstein's Factory (2)
1	Pigg Lane 10
7	Pottergate 101 (2) 92 (1) 45 (1) 17 (1) 10 (1) Gable end - Emms Yard (1)
5	Peacock Street 9 (1) 11 (1) 14 (3)
5	Redwell Street Church Alley on School Wall (2) Caretaker's House (2) Haldenstein's (1)
6	St Giles 18 (2) 30 (1) 33 (1) 32 (2)
4	St Benedicts 61-63 (1) (2) 74 (1)
2	St George Street Stonemasons Yard, [Square] 20 (2)
1	St Georges 160 (2)
6	St Martins Oak Street 19-21 (4) St Marys Silk Mill (1) St Martins Oak Street Flats (1) One lost in the demolition
4	Palace Street 17-19 (4)
2	St Stephen's Street 1-3 (2)
5	St Faiths Lane outside arch (2) inside arch (1) centre of Lane (1) and Boundary Stone on PAC wall (1)
3	Magdalene Street 18 (1) 20 (2)
1	Queen Street 7 not fixed (1)
2	Muspole Street 21 (2)
3	Theatre Street Butchers Court (3)

2   ditto   back of 11 (2)
2   Thorne Lane Lower Square Stone Marks (2)
2   ditto   Morris [Morriss] Court (2)
1   Timberhill 33 (1)
3   Westwick Street wall near pump (2) 62 (1)
2   ditto   Bullards Bottling Store (2)
2   Wensum Street Maids Head (2)
5   Westlegate 5 (1) 3a (1) Gable end of 7 (3)
2   Strangers Hall (2)
5   City Engineers (5)
5   Private Holding (5)

November 1934
TOTAL 185

[The above entries are followed by these extra details:-]

Theatre Street Plain - Assembly House
4   South-west Corner
1   Safety Staircase

(Elm Hill)

5   Towlers Court on old Clock House (4) on end of
       left house (1) (demolished 12/34)
3   Barrack Street 87 (3) demolished 1/1935. Plates in charge of owner   at
       Bull Close S. Armes.
2   Whitefriars Monastery remains in charge of Jarrolds   6/1934
4   Oak Street 19, 21 (demolished 3/1935) the plates in charge of
       owners, Messrs Bagshaw.

All the above sites listed by Mr Read have been visited (not to mention revisited) and carefully studied in the hope that some markers would still be in their 1934/35 noted positions. Some were found, but many were not.

    Several old place names and locations simply do not exist today or, if they do, the new area bearing the old name is not in the original location. Mind you, I have to be glad that the odd old name lives on here and there. I feel strongly that retaining place names and their connection to locations, is vital, being important factors linking us to our rich heritage.

    It is ironic that while Mr Read was busy noting down the extra entries at the end of his Index, he was obliged to comment that, in the space of only four months, sites had been demolished at Towler's Court, Barrack Street and Oak Street. Although the plates on these razed buildings seemed to be

46

safe, at least temporarily, the worry had to be who was going to secure their eventual safe storage? To prove the point, none of these displaced plates can be conclusively traced today.

I am particularly distressed about the reference to number 87 Barrack Street. Mr Read photographed the 3 plates there. In his book they look to be hanging on wires fixed to a corrugated iron fence. They were all for the Pockthorpe area: two for the Hamlet, (1817 & 1831) and one for St James, Pockthorpe (1824) in which delightful little church I was baptised, confirmed and later, in 1965, appointed organist. I was last to hold that position. The building is now the Puppet Theatre. The 1817 plate is rather lavishly over-decorated with crowns, flowers and a classically stylised Greek female figure.

Just a very quick glance down the list of locations known in 1934 to Mr Read, highlights the missing sites today. Pipeburners Yard (off Bull Close Road), Charing Cross numbers 12, 13, and 14, Coburg Street, (behind St Stephen's Street and now amidst new shopping development) Cowgate numbers 120 and 128, part of Church Street (now William Booth Street), the Corn Hall (Exchange Street, part of Messrs Jarrolds' shop), Hungate Museum (now closed), Peacock Street (off Fishergate), Stonemasons Yard [Court] (off Pitt Street), Butchers Court (off Theatre Street), Thorn Lane Lower Square (off King Street), and Morriss Court (off King Street) are all gone forever, at least as Mr Read would have known them.

APPENDIX B

EXISTING NORWICH BOUNDARY MARKERS 2007
Locations alphabetically by parish

All Saints

1778   12 All Saint's Green, gable end (behind drainpipe).
1778   Bridewell Museum (ex number 7 Westlegate).
1818   12 All Saint's Green, gable end (behind drainpipe).
1818   Westlegate, Messrs Evans' shop.
1818   33 Timber Hill. Messrs Ward & Wright.
1818   Bridewell Museum (ex number 7 Westlegate).

St Andrew *(Note the X cross, symbol of his martyrdom).*
1813   4 Princes Street (unique shape for this parish).
1832   4 Princes Street.
1832   School Lane (Bedford Street end).
1832   Blackfriars Hall, Elm Hill Buttress (well concealed).
1832   Blackfriars Hall, Elm Hill Buttress, facing Elm Hill mounted very high above pavement.

St Augustine
    1811   57-61, Pitt Street.
    1826   57-61, Pitt Street.
    1826   Bridewell Museum (ex 92 Calvert Street).

St Bartholomew
    1811 Hamlet of St Bartholomew, 'Royal Arch Court', Earlham Road, by Grapes Hill pedestrian bridge. Only example known for this parish.
    Note the central symbol of crossed knives by which implements this saint was martyred.
    Due to be fixed to new building March 2007 after demolition removal from this site (ex-Duff Morgan's garage) in 2005)

St Benedict

    1854   A.C.Leigh's, St Benedict Street, (latest date of any extant plate marker in original position, in Norwich).

    1854   Bridewell Museum (original location unknown).

St Clement *(Note the anchor, symbol of his martyrdom).*

    1809   The Merchants Public House, Colegate, (obscured by drain-pipe).

    1809   19 Colegate. (Octagon House).

    1809   Bridewell Museum, (original location unknown, stamped IV on the reverse). -

    1821   Bridewell Museum, (original location unknown, stamped II on the reverse). -

    1821   19 Colegate. (Octagon House).

    1821   Formerly Messrs Looses, Magdalen Street, (mounted high above pavement).

    1821   The Merchants Public House, Colegate, (obscured by drain-pipe).

St Edmund, Fishergate
  1800   Bridewell Museum, (original location unknown).
  1829   Bridewell Museum, (ex garden of Gurney Court).

St Etheldreda *(Plates made by Charles Foster?)*.
  1786   168 King Street.
  1786   The Music House, King Street.

St George, Colegate

1802   50 Colegate (previously Norvic Shoe Co. – now Norwich Union).
1821   21 Colegate.
1821   57-61, Pitt Street.
1821   The Merchants Public House, Colegate, (obscured by drainpipe).
1821   50 Colegate (previously Norvic Shoe Co. – now Norwich Union).
1821   Bridewell Museum - 3 plates; one marked 'Golden Dog lane' [No 15?], others stamped I and X on reverse - but no original locations identified.

St George, Tombland

1748   St Faith's Lane, opposite number 7 (very rare stone marker).
1748   Planning & Conservation, City Hall, 2 markers (original locations unknown. NB figure 1 is upside down!). See illustration page 66.
1777   16 Princes Street, (interesting shape for this year).
1777   Entrance Arch St Faith's Lane, fronting Tombland end
1777   Maid's Head Hotel, Wensum Street, (obscured by drainpipe).
1828   Entrance Arch St Faith's Lane, fronting Tombland end. (Only 4 feet above pavement level and excellent for scrutiny).
1828   Inner Courtyard of Messrs Brown & Co. Queen's Street.

St Giles

1710   Coach & Horses Public House, Bethel Street, (shared very rare stone marker).

1772   Salvation Army 'archway', St Giles Street, (shared very rare stone marker - only a fragment remains).

1772   Micawber's Tavern, Pottergate (shared very rare stone marker. See also St Margaret page 56).

1806   54 Bethel Street. Recessed into rear garden wall.

1814   Salvation Army 'archway', St Giles Street.

1814   Coach & Horses Public House, Bethel Street.

1829   54 Bethel Street.

1829   Coach & Horses Public House, Bethel Street.

1829   Salvation Army 'archway', St Giles Street.

1829   33 St Giles Street.

1829   37 St Giles Street (on side wall at rear of property).

St Gregory

1772   Salvation Army 'archway', St Giles Street, (shared left hand segment of very rare stone marker). Note small letter 'Y' above first 7 and compare with 1828 plate for parish style.

1828   Bridewell Museum, 2 markers (original locations unknown).

1828   Westwick Street, Charing Cross end, (underneath heavy growth of overhanging ivy, quite difficult to find).

1829   32, St Giles Street

St John, Maddermarket *(Note the shell symbol of Saint John the Baptist)*.
1829   10 Pottergate, by Bagley's Court, (mounted very high).
1829   Above entrance to Strangers' Hall Museum, Charing Cross.
NB Letter I used for J[ohn]. This plate is very easy to observe.
1829   Bridewell Museum. Marked on reverse 'Removed from Exchange Street, 1955'. (Possibly from old Corn Hall).

St John, Timberhill *(Note central device of overlapping leaves represents a 'timber-hill')*.
1826   Bridewell Museum. 3 markers. Original locations: one is marked '15 Golden Ball .... [Street?]'; another ex number 7 Westlegate and the third is unknown.
1826   18 Golden Ball Street. Opposite The Woolpack. This plate is beautifully painted and well worth seeing.
1826   37 All Saints Green.

St Julian (*'Mother Julian of Norwich' 1342-c.1416 lived here in a reclusive's cell attached to the church. It is believed that the parchments on which she recorded her spiritual visions, came from the next parish of St Peter Parmentergate. See also page 60).*
- 1789   The Music House, King Street.
- 1800   168 King Street.
- 1825   168 King Street.
- 1825   The Music House, King Street. (NB The letter 'J' for Julian is represented as a letter I on all four examples, following the fashion of the time).

St Laurence (*Note the wonderful central device representing the grid-iron on which this Saint was martyred).*
- 1806   Bridewell Museum, 2 markers (one ex Westwick Street).
- 1806   Bridewell Museum (original location unknown).
- 1806   Westwick Street, Charing Cross end (beneath ivy).

St Margaret *(Note the central device on the 1779 plate is likely to be a palm, which was one of her saintly symbols).*

1772 Micawber's Tavern, Pottergate, (left segment of shared very rare stone marker. The right side is for St Giles).

1779 Bridewell Museum ex Westwick Street, old Bullard's Brewery site. (NB The Figure 1 is upside down, not unusual on other parish plates.)

St Martin-at-Oak *(Named after a large tree once in grounds).*

1824 Bridewell Museum, rescued by the author during demolition of the then Courtauld's Factory situated on Oak Street, in March 1983. (Only example known for this parish.)

St Mary, Coslany
1792   Bridewell Museum (stamped XI on reverse).
1812   Bridewell Museum, 3 markers (original locations unknown). One stamped XIV on reverse with left edge of plate clipped away. Two others are stamped XIII and XXIII respectively on reverses.

St Michael & All Angels, Coslany *(Locally known as 'St Miles' which derives from the latin for 'soldier', as in St Michael's army of angels).*
1729   Bridewell Museum (ex St Martin-at-Oak Street), legend pierced through flat metal sheet, mounted on wooden block. Unique design, and oldest dated plate extant in Norwich. Reverse of block is stamped III.
1791   38-44 Council Flats, Oak Street.
1791   7-13 Council Flats, Rosemary Lane.

St Michael-at-Plea(s) *(So called as the church was once used as the venue for the Archdeacon's ecclesiastical court, where pleas were heard).*
1756   Bridewell Museum (original location unknown).
1806   Planning & Conservation Dept. City Hall (original location unknown).
1821   Church Cottage, rear of St Michael-at-Plea Church
1821   New flats by Church House, behind Church.
1836   Bridewell Museum, (original location unknown).

St Michael-at-Thorn *(Named after the very high thorn hedges which once surrounded the church yard).*
1821   Bridewell Museum. Only extant plate for this parish.

St Peter Hungate *(Likely to derive from 'Hound-Gate'. See page 41 for explanation).*

- 1742 Bridewell Museum, 2 markers (original locations unknown - plates stamped V and VI respectively on reverse).
- 1814 39 Elm Hill. The Jade Tree.
- 1814 Bridewell Museum, stamped VII on reverse, (original location unknown).
- 1814 Church House, rear of St Michael-at-Plea Church.
- 1814 28 Elm Hill. Elm Hill Antiques.
- 1814 4 Princes Street.

- 1834 Bridewell Museum, 2 markers (original locations unknown - one only is stamped, IX on reverse).
- 1834 Church Cottage, rear of St Michael-at-Plea Church.
- 1834 Church House, rear of St Michael-at-Plea Church.
- 1834 4 Princes Street.
- 1834 28 Elm Hill. Elm Hill Antiques.
- 1834 Messrs Eversheds, Paston House, Princes Street.
- 1834 16 Princes Street.
- 1834 39 Elm Hill. The Jade Tree.
- 1834 Bridewell Museum. White lettering on Black ground.

St Peter Mancroft *(Named from 'Magna Crofta' – St Peter's in the large field. Note the saint's crossed keys).*

    1710   Coach & Horses Public House, Bethel Street, (shared very rare stone marker with the right hand portion belonging to the parish of St Giles).

    1813   Coach & Horses Public House, Bethel Street.

    1813   Rear of Assembly House, Theatre Street.

    1827   Bridewell Museum (original location unknown).

    1827   52 Bethel Street.

    1827   William Booth Street, (formerly Church Street).

    1827   Rear of Assembly House, Theatre Street.

    1827   Coach & Horses Public House, Bethel Street.

St Peter par Mentergate also per Mountergate *(Name derives from 'parmentering'- the making of parchment paper which thrived here in medieval times. The name is now written Parmentergate. Note the saint's crossed keys)*

    1827   Bridewell Museum (original location unknown).

St Saviour, Stump Cross *(So called by reason of the stone cross, which stood near the church at the junction of Botolph Street, now defunct. Note that the 1816 plate shows the cross on a plinth/stump).*

1801   Bridewell Museum, (ex 36 Calvert Street). Rescued by the author in 1983.

1816   Bridewell Museum, (ex 36 Calvert Street). Rescued by the author in 1983.

1824   Bridewell Museum, (ex rear of 79, Magdalen Street).

1824   Doughty's Hospital (pedestrian way, by flyover).

1824   Doughty's Hospital by private car park in grounds.

1832   Bridewell Museum (ex 36 Calvert Street). Rescued by the author in 1983.

1832   Doughty's Hospital (pedestrian way, by flyover).

1832   Doughty's Hospital by private car park in grounds.

St Simon & St Jude
    1842   28 Elm Hill. Elm Hill Antiques. See also Appendix C under Elm
            Hill
    1842   41 Elm Hill. Turner Brown Antiques.
    1842   Wensum Street. Maid's Head Hotel (partially obscured by
            drainpipe).
    1842   Bridewell Museum, (original location unknown - stamped VIII
            on reverse).
(NB the letter 'J' for Jude is represented as a letter I on all
four examples, following the fashion of the time).

St Stephen *(Note the 1820 ram's head - a martyr's symbol).*
    1804   Rear of Assembly House, Theatre Street.
    1820   Rear of Assembly House, Theatre Street.
    1834   1 The Crescent, Chapelfield. On rear wall of house.
    1834   In church strongbox, c/o P.C.C., not on view to
            public, (possibly ex Butchers Court - now demolished).
    1834   Bridewell Museum (ex Messrs Boston's Clothiers of Farmer's
            Avenue. Placed in museum 1974).

St Swithin

1809   74 St Benedict Street   (only example known for this parish).
Detail enhanced by hand as plate lettering is impaired by multiple over-
painting. The symbol may be two crossed nails, which were
miraculously loosened from holding two rings on his tomb when
touched by a sick man, who was instantly cured.

APPENDIX C

Locations where several boundary markers may be seen at one site
[NB the markers are metal plates, unless otherwise stated]

Bethel Street
Coach & Horses Public House
Four Plates & One Shared Stone Marker dated 1710*
St Peter Mancroft 1710*, 1813 & 1827
St Giles 1710*, 1814 & 1829

Colegate Street
The Merchants Public House
St Clement 1809 & 1821
St George, Colegate 1821

Elm Hill
39 The Jade Tree
St Peter Hungate 1814 & 1834

41 Turner Brown Antiques
St Simon & St Jude 1842

28 Elm Hill Antiques
St Peter Hungate 1814 & 1834
St Simon & St Jude 1842 N.B. This plate is not in the correct position. It should be sited on the right of the two SPH 1814 /1834 markers at this address

King Street
Number 168
St Etheldreda 1786
St Julian 1800 & 1825

The Music House
St Etheldreda 1786
St Julian 1825

Pitt Street, 57-61
St Augustine 1811 & 1826
St George Colegate 1821

Princes Street
Number 4
St Andrew 1813 & 1832
St Peter Hungate 1814 & 1834

Redwell Street (Church Alley)
Church House
St Peter Hungate 1814 & 1834

Theatre Street
The Assembly House (Rear)
St Peter Mancroft 1813 & 1827
St Stephen 1804 & 1820

Tombland
Entrance arch leading to St Faith's Lane
St George Tombland 1777 & 1828

Wensum Street
The Maid's Head Hotel,
St George Tombland 1777
St Simon & St Jude 1842

APPENDIX D

Plates lost in recent years

St George Tombland

1748 Plate sold by auction in Yorkshire November 2006. Details of provenance and previous and new owner withheld by the auctioneers. Sadly has to be classed as 'precise whereabouts unknown.' (See page 3 for circumstances.)

St Michael, Coslany, (St Miles)

1791   50 Colegate (previously Norvic Shoe Co. now Norwich Union).

1827   50 Colegate (previously Norvic Shoe Co. now Norwich Union).

Removed during building refurbishment in the 1990s. Efforts to trace items through Norwich Union and others have proved fruitless.

St Peter Mancroft

1827   Mounted on stair landing inside Assembly House, Theatre Street.

Sadly, this plate perished in the devastating fire at the Assembly House on 12 April 1995. Other examples of this to be found elsewhere. See Appendix B.   See also St Stephen entry below.

St Peter par Mentergate (per Mountergate)

1827   Previously sited on Menzies Wholesale Warehouse,   Cathedral Street - whereabouts now unknown.

This plate was removed c. 1992/93, before the current owners moved into these premises. Attempts to trace it have been fruitless. An identical (and unique) plate is stored in the Bridewell Museum.

St Stephen
1804 Mounted on stair landing inside Assembly House, Theatre Street.
1820 Mounted on stair landing inside Assembly House, Theatre Street.
1834 Mounted on stair landing inside Assembly House, Theatre Street.
Sadly, these three plates all perished in the fire, which devastated the
Assembly House 12 April 1995. Other examples of these dates can be found
elsewhere.   See Appendix B.

Picture Credits

Photographs on pages 15, 16, 20, 37 and 43 and on the back cover are published by kind permission of Eastern Counties Newspapers, having first appeared in the *Evening News*.

Ordnance Survey has given permission for the maps opposite page 1 and on page 26 to be printed.

Pictures on the title page and pages 9, 11 and 21 were first printed in The *East Anglian* magazine, now no longer in circulation, and copyright has not been traced.

All other photographs are in the author's private collection and may not be reproduced without his permission.